FIRST EDITION

ADAPT AND OVERCOME

ESSAYS ON THE STUDENT VETERAN EXPERIENCE

by Mary E. McNaughton-Cassill

UNIVERSITY OF TEXAS—SAN ANTONIO

cognella®
academic publishing

Bassim Hamadeh, CEO and Publisher

Michael Simpson, Vice President of Acquisitions and Sales

Jamie Giganti, Senior Managing Editor

Jess Busch, Senior Graphic Designer

Marissa Applegate, Senior Field Acquisitions Editor

Natalie Lakosil, Licensing Manager

Kat Ragudos, Interior Designer

First published in the United States of America in 2016 by Cognella, Inc.

Cover photo taken by Aaron Cassill.

Printed in the United States of America

ISBN: 978-1-62661-605-9 / 978-1-62661-606-6 (br)

www.cognella.com   800-200-3908

CONTENTS

UNIT 5
CIVILIANS: WORKING TO HELP VETERANS SUCCEED IN COLLEGE

DEDICATION

This book is dedicated to the military service members who devote their time, energy, and lives to protecting our country, and in particular to the veterans who took time out of their very busy lives to share their experiences in this volume.

I would also like to thank and acknowledge the following people:

Jessica Knott, the editor extraordinaire who provided the idea for this book, and who was invaluable in helping me to initiate and organize this project.

Sandra Pahl, a former UTSA and UT–Austin student, now a clinical psychologist in the US Navy, who generously reviewed the manuscript and shared her insights throughout the process.

Carolyn Cassill, my daughter, a graduate of UT–Austin and aspiring neuropsychologist, who carefully read, edited, and organized all of the essays in this volume, and who also served as my personal technology assistant!

My daughter Julia Cassill, sister Caren Edwards, and husband Aaron Cassill for helping me "mind all the gaps" that arose over the course of this project.

PREFACE

The Veteran Student Narrative
Mary McNaughton-Cassill

Humans have long been storytellers, whether they were drawing on cave walls, writing about great battles, listening to travelling storytellers, or singing about romance. Although animals can learn from each other through observation, sounds, and nonverbal signals, our language capabilities enable us to share complex, abstract information and technological expertise with individuals and across generations. In fact, it is hard to underestimate the value of human storytelling as a means of transmitting survival techniques, fostering innovation, and sharing cultural beliefs. Storytelling also enables us to envision the future and talk about the past, thereby allowing us to move back and forth on the continuum of time. With the advent of technology, our ability to convey those stories has expanded exponentially. Radio, television, and the Internet make it easy for people around the world to share their stories and experiences. On a personal level, social media, including Facebook, Twitter, blogs, etc., provides us with a means of sharing our personal stories with others. The fact that we can edit, alter, and rewrite versions of ourselves is one of the main reasons these media are so popular.

Psychologists and biologists argue that our brains are predisposed to be social, and that we remember facts better when they are part of a story, particularly if the narrative involves arousal and emotion. This tension helps us remain focused, while the feelings help us stay engaged. Certainly, the entertainment value of storytelling has never been higher. Never before have so many people had access to so many sophisticated stories via television, movies, theater, music, dance, the internet, and electronic and paper books. But, paradoxically, this surfeit of options means that we never feel we have enough time to see and do everything, and have to find ways to choose what we do want to view based on both our individual, and cultural views and beliefs. In short, when picking the stories we want to consume, we are in affect, also writing our own life story.

Since the 1970s, psychologists have been studying how the stories we tell ourselves shape our worlds, our relationships, our expectations, and our emotional states. This field, often referred to as narrative therapy, is based on the idea that our storytelling brains are constantly recording, revising, and developing our personal screenplays. As we move through life, we frame and reframe our experiences, change our attributions about our choices, and revise our memories each time we revisit them. This is due in part to the fact that the brain is predisposed to seek closure, to make logical assumptions, and to fill in gaps when we are missing information. Without this ability, we would have difficulty functioning in our complex three-dimensional world, where much of the sensory information we take in is incomplete, our future is often unpredictable, and our present is restricted to our personal awareness. For many of us, our childhood memories are less an accurate personal memory and more a memory of the stories those around us have relayed. Of course, this ability to fill in the blanks also means that we can choose to focus on details that support our belief system and to ignore those that don't. If we have settled on a particular theme for an event, or our life story, we may then organize our recollections to reflect our sense of ourselves—as a victim, a warrior, a loner etc. From a therapeutic point of view, narrative therapy approaches often attempt to identify how an individual's self-narrative is helping or hindering his or her psychological adjustment, and how it can be used to alter or shape new and more adaptive views of old events and assumptions. Many of our returning service members have painful stories to tell, and there is increasing attention on whether telling these stories can help them deal with their anxiety and stress. For example, the work of James Pennebaker (2004) suggests that simply writing about events in your life, whether or not anyone else reads what you write, can help people process and cope with traumatic memories.

Another part of the story that is less frequently told is how veterans adjust after leaving the military. We hear about spectacular successes and failures, but what about those in the middle? Many veterans reestablish their lives, returning to their homes, families, and communities. In some cases, they take up their premilitary careers. Other vets use their benefits to return to school. While in theory this can seem like a logical next step, on a personal level, this may not be an easy transition. Veterans often feel as though they are in a strange new world. Certainly, the military and academia are vastly different cultures, with their own sets of rules, practices, goals and stories. Consequently, veterans may struggle to find their way around campus, and the campus community often doesn't understand what they are going through, let alone how to help them.

This book will explore these topics through the eyes of student veterans, their classmates, and the faculty and staff who work with them at the University of Texas at San Antonio. This urban campus is the largest in the San Antonio metro region, which itself is often referred to as "Military City USA" because it is home to Lackland Air Force Base, Ft. Sam Houston (Army), Camp Bullis (Marine Corps), and the Brooke Army Medical Center and the Wounded Warrior Program. Furthermore, Naval Air Station Corpus Christi is only a short three-hour drive away. In the fall of 2012, close to 1,500 of the almost 31,000 students at UTSA were veterans. Almost a third of those were female. Veterans were found in every college of the university and at every level, from freshman to graduate student. As such, veteran students make up a significant portion of UTSA's campus community.

The goal of the project is to give readers a sense of the diversity of our current veterans, as well as of the similarities in their experiences as they leave the military and return to school. Participants have been given free rein to write about their early lives, their military careers, their academic experiences, and their future aspirations. We hope that these stories will enable the friends and families of veterans to better understand what they are going through and how to support their academic journeys. We also hope to share insight gained from the veterans' stories with faculty, staff, administrators, and other college students, and in turn to have members of each of those groups reflect on their experiences working with (and in some cases, also being) a veteran.

1

CHOOSING TO SERVE

JASON FRAZIER
MARINES

Jason's quick wit, subtle humor, and impressive writing skills belie his tough childhood in Baltimore. He readily credits his experiences as a Marine for helping him escape the world of drugs and prison that captured many of his friends. However, as an outstanding graduate of the Honors College at UTSA and current Psychology Graduate student, he has become a role model for other members of both his military and biological families.

Let's start at the beginning. I always find that helps. I celebrate three birthdays every year. The first one is the day I was physically brought into the world. The second marks the day I stepped onto the yellow footprints at Parris Island that signify the first steps toward becoming a member of the Marine Corps. Last, but not least, I, and all Marines, have our ancestral birthday on 10 November. I say this to emphasize my veteran status as well as to introduce myself. This triad of birthdays helps to emphasize how complex human beings, and their experiences, can be.

This is especially true in college and the military. The possibilities for stress, change, growth, and fulfillment are all present in both of these settings. A person can go into either college or the military and come out completely different. Now, try to imagine going through both.

For me, both of these experiences altered how I behaved socially more than in any other realm. In general, I am fairly smart, decently fit, and mostly responsible. However, if you look at my social life at different stages—before the Marines, before college, and after graduating—you might as well be looking at three different lives. Each of these lives has followed a pattern of improvement in social functioning and adaptability. Because of this, I'd like to offer the benefit of my experience—particularly my thoughts, feelings, and theories about the social aspects of being a veteran, both in and out of college.

My purpose for writing this is to emphasize the importance of dual-sided social support. By dual-sided, I mean support and interaction between both those above and below an individual on a social or professional level. In some ways, this model resembles something that is already familiar for many veterans. I believe that this model allows for an easier transition to, and a more fulfilling experience during, college. It also allows for multiple methods of social support and interaction.

First, let's examine the difference between a Permanent Change of Station (PCS) and an EAS (End of Active Service). Both of these activities are defined by major changes in livelihood (location, living arrangements, social support, and familiarity of systems). PCS is mandatory for a vast majority of military personnel (from basic training to the permanent duty station). Reenlisting normally includes a significant PCS and can involve a major change within a similar system of peers, supervisors (or mentors), and subordinates. A PCS can be seen as beneficial because the individual is moving from one established support system (i.e., rank structure) to another—no individual effort is required to create a new structure. The system picks you up from a group that you know and plops you down into a group you do not know, and all of the support and responsibility structures are automatically in place for the service man or woman.

EAS is just the opposite. Leaving the military can literally destroy every social or professional support structure an individual has worked years to create and maintain. In other words, EAS removes almost everything a veteran is accustomed to or has accomplished. Most times, EAS is seen as more enjoyable and fulfilling at first. I know it was with me. I was ecstatic when I was able to remove all of the trash in my life related to the Big Green Weenie (as we like to call the Marine Corps). However, when you look at the bigger picture, there is a huge amount of unfamiliar change and lack of support, so that first rush of happiness may not last long. Gap-time between enlistments and help from specific military support groups (VFW, VA, etc.) is a prime example of the huge amount of effort needed to relieve the troubling aspects of an EAS.

Let's take some time to break down the effects of ending a military career. If EAS is so great, why do so many higher-ranking military members have at least a one-year gap-time in their careers? I think that maybe it is not all as bright and shiny as many service men and women paint it to be. EAS can remove all current, primary social or professional support while simultaneously gutting all major activities related to enrichment and personal fulfillment. Many others and I have personally experienced this effect.

While I was in the Marines, I was a leader, a teacher, an avid exerciser, a role model, and a great socializer. Within one month of EAS, I had no job, one or two friends, and no one and nothing to teach. I rarely exercised, and spent very little time with other people. The months and weeks before I EAS'ed, I was so excited to leave, but only a few weeks after I had left, I was frustrated that I had lost everything upon which I had built my identity. At that point I was already accepted into a college, but even the possible adventure of moving across the county to start out on a whole new life just tasted like dust in my mouth.

I, like many others, cannot count the times I thought about reenlisting the first two years after my EAS. It was at least once a day. I missed my brothers in uniform. I missed how I knew what I needed to do every single day. I loathed how ambiguous, slow, and lazy all of these nasty civilians acted. I felt a burning need in my soul to be active, intense, and on point at all times. After much reflection, I realize now what I really craved then was support. I needed both a mentor and an apprentice. Only after I had gained dual-sided support did I understand how and why I had these troubles. The next logical questions are: What is dual-sided support? Why does it matter? Why should anyone care, especially someone as overwhelmed as a military veteran going to college? I hope I can answer these questions.

I have found that much in life follows a basic principle: as it is above, so it is below. Most people seek out self-fulfillment both above and below. Humans wish to be challenged and provide positive motivation and challenges for others. This can be done, and often *is* done, by teaching and modeling more adaptive and positive behavior. Most of us behave better and seek out higher goals when viewed by others who have power over us or people over whom we have power. In other words, you may smoke and joke with your friends (peers), but when your boss or your subordinates come around, you best be on point and squared away.

Next, we must apply the lens that reveals how humans are social beings, and that many pine for acceptance, acclaim, and fulfillment. Support from both mentor and apprentice figures fulfills all of these desires on multiple levels, above and below. True mentors lead and teach their apprentices (here, the vet) by accepting who the student is as a person and motivating him or her towards individualized goals. Being a strong mentor and teacher provides social and professional fulfillment. Lastly, both mentors and apprentices provide acclaim (or external sources of accreditation, positivity, and status).

Now, dear reader, you must be thinking, "Why do I care about some structure of social support that does not even apply to me?" Well, again, I hope to provide a good answer to this question. If you have any experience with the military, be it direct or indirect, you know about the rank structure. By default, dual-sided social support is built into the military rank structure. This social trend is not only created but also ingrained and enforced by, and within, military culture. This means that veterans are already familiar with (and perhaps expect) this form of social and professional support when they enter a new environment. When this network is not found or doesn't function as expected, transition and adjustment for a veteran or military member can become much more difficult. However, if this type of support is found, shifted into, or created by a vet in a new environment, adjustment can become easier and natural. As with anything, if you are familiar with or comfortable in a situation, you will generally perform better. Therefore, my belief is that veterans or active military benefit and even thrive with dual-sided social support because they have experienced its ingrained nature during their military careers.

As with the military rank structure, vets occupy just one point in a complex web. Also, because of the universal nature of the rank structure, military members can easily shift from one section of the web to another with minimal stress or effort. For example, if you walk from your workplace to your barracks, you are still expected to respect the rank structure of all individuals within the barracks, and they are expected to respect your rank. This does not prevent social or professional support in the barracks. In fact, it can encourage socializing, as a series of social standards already exists between ranks that enables these relationships.

In this way, it can be beneficial for a veteran to create multiple "webs" he or she can shift between to fulfill his or her needs or wants. You can have one for schoolwork, one for socializing, one for exercising, one for professional development, etc. This does not mean that these networks are mutually exclusive, and it does not mean that you have to be close to every person in the network. Each social relationship can be as strong or as weak as desired, and can go in either (or both) directions (above and below).

This may be a difficult thing to explain theoretically, so let's pull back to reality a bit. Say you have an acquaintance you met at the gym. This acquaintance seems to be nice and a decent person, so you contact him. Now, let's suppose this acquaintance has a few friends who are equally as nice and are all decent people, but they are all younger and less experienced than you, due to your time in the military. This would provide you with a unique, strong social network of peers and/or apprentices for socializing and perhaps schoolwork.

Let's now also suppose that you and one of your new friends need some clarity about an assignment from a professor. If you were to take the initiative in this situation—asking the professor about the assignment, continuing communication with the professor, and relaying that information while assisting your friend—you would have just created a dual-sided social/professional network. Just like with rank structure, seeking out apprentices and mentors allows you to become a medium between those with experience and power (mentors) and those without (apprentices), while simultaneously providing and receiving guidance from both sides. In this way, you enter a familiar role while working on the skills and knowledge you need to succeed in a new environment.

Now that I have explained a little about what dual-sided support is, I can begin to explain how to create the web of support. First, let's look above and focus on finding and choosing true mentors. What makes a mentor a good fit? For what traits should we search? Where or at whom should we look? Two phrases I heard during my time in the Marines come to mind. First, respect the rank, not the person. Second, learn the good and leave the bad. This means that in all interactions with those who have some form of power over you, be respectful of their power (rank) even if you feel they are not good people. Second, learn the good and leave the bad. Look for positive traits to imitate and model in mentors, and leave (or don't imitate) things that you don't agree with or that don't work. Using both my experience and these general rules, I have come up with a few general traits that help to identify true, positive mentors.

True mentors show congruence, positive regard, empathy, usefulness, and focus. Each one of these traits is equally important, but not each one will be a mentor's strength. I have had mentors who were extremely empathetic and congruent, but maybe were not so useful or focused. On the flip side, I have had extremely useful and focused mentors who were horribly incongruent, lacked empathy, and showed no form of positive regard. I learned something good from each of my mentors, but I took away some bad things from them as well.

Each trait is important for true mentorship, but all of them (except congruence, which should be universal) are associated with social or professional mentorship. This is not to say that all mentors must have some form of each trait, but social or professional mentors provide a greater benefit to apprentices when their focus is clear.

As I said earlier, congruence is universal, so I'll start there. Simply put, congruence means speaking and acting in consistent ways, regardless of the situation or people involved—"do as I do." A congruent mentor shows little to no difference in behavior between apprentices, colleagues or peers, and their own mentors. A congruent individual behaves similarly in every situation, which makes them authentic and true to themselves and others. Congruence is important for mentors because it destroys any chance of favoritism or bias during teaching or instruction.

The social traits of mentorship include positive regard and empathy. Positive regard is showing support and care without judgment. It enables a mentor to see an individual's strengths and abilities without judging their actions. This allows a mentor to encourage an individual (the apprentice) to set appropriate goals which will emphasize their strengths and push them towards a better quality of life.

Empathy is of the utmost importance for a social mentor. This is the ability to see or relate to another individual's perspective or lifestyle, and it also involves the ability to send and receive proper emotional cues. Empathy allows mentors to directly relate to their apprentices because they can remember (or imagine) how it feels to be in a position of needing help. Empathy allows basic social relationships to bloom, and without it proper social communication will be greatly impaired on both sides of the relationship.

On the professional side of things, mentors should show usefulness and focus. Usefulness is any knowledge, skill, or ability that a mentor can teach an apprentice. Usefulness can be every area of life, but the more a mentor's skills match your goals, the more useful the mentor will be. Usefulness is paramount for professional mentors; if a professional mentor is not useful, then he or she will not teach you the skills you need to succeed in your profession.

Focus refers to general organization and motivation. This relates to both teaching and personality. Mentors should be dedicated to their fields of study and to their students. Additionally, their behavior should positively affect their apprentices by modeling the organization and drive they want to encourage their students to develop. For example, if a professor is consistently slovenly, late, disorganized, and droll during interactions or lectures, that professor is more than likely not so hot. However, if a professor is enthusiastic, punctual, well groomed, orderly, interactive, and dynamic during lectures, he's likely to be a much better teacher. Focus is not absolutely vital for professional mentors, but a focused mentor will be much more effective at teaching information and skills.

Now that I have defined several of the things I look for in strong mentors, I would like to offer advice about how to find such people. Normally, from a military standpoint, mentors are arbitrarily thrust into a person's life. This mentorship can start in boot camp and carry all the way through to retirement. However, mentors who are found, rather than assigned, have the potential to be more beneficial.

In my life, the first screening method I used to find mentors was peer reviews—I used information from others of a similar status to locate a highly respected and appreciated mentor. In the military, this usually involves smoking and joking with your squad-mates to find out which NCO or officer actually cares. When thinking about college, finding a mentor involves talking to fellow students, seeking their opinions about professors and tuning into the gossip about assignments, level of caring, and general attitudes. On top of this, any professional recommendations or referrals may also be useful here, since this is another form of peer review. I have always found that a person's reputation is fairly accurate if it is gotten from multiple, reliable sources. As such, I have tried to reach out to many of my friends, or their friends, to gather information and opinions about a potential mentor in whom I have some interest. This use of my social web or network has been extremely beneficial because, before a mentor gets to me, he or she needs to be recognized by someone who is already in my circle.

Next, I like to examine a mentor's interest or personality. I ask, "What do they like or dislike? How do they talk to others? Can I fit into that?" These questions check to see if the potential mentor and I are like-minded. This is especially important for professional mentors, as I wish to learn more in my areas of interest. At the same time, it is important that mentors and apprentices have similar personalities, worldviews, and mindsets. Without this parallel, mentors will never be able to provide the best forms of social support, guidance, or "upwards pull" (going up the web or network to a better or more connected spot). I have found that I am most happy with mentors who share similar motivations and interests as I, and these people have been extremely supportive and motivating for me.

Interests go hand in hand with ability. To me, a mentor with ability is one who has enough time to teach and help. No time means no help. This is pretty simple. I always try to make sure any mentor with whom I want to work has both the availability and the skills to teach or assist me. This includes any type of skill, whether it is physical, emotional, social, or professional.

An example here would probably be helpful. Let's look at learning a physical skill, since most military personnel have learned at least one physical skill during their careers. I learned how to shoot when I joined the Marines, so that experience will provide a good way to illustrate my point. When learning to perform a skill well, it is important that a person finds a mentor who has the time to teach as well as the skills needed. For me, my SNCO was excellent at shooting and ran multiple ranges for my unit. Also, I knew he had the time to help, as he was in my section and was personally responsible for supervising and conducting the ranges. After talking about shooting with both my SNCO and others, I knew that he would be able and willing to spend all the time I needed to help me learn to shoot well. This was a prime opportunity for me, and I jumped on it as soon as possible. Now, I am very confident in my ability with many weapons systems, and I have passed on much of the training my SNCO taught me to my friends and peers.

The last thing I scrutinize when I am searching for a mentor is communication skills. Ideally, I want a mentor with strong communication skills and a low response time. In my opinion, there is no use in spending time working and learning from a mentor who cannot communicate thoughts or opinions in time to help me. I need a mentor with whom I can speak. Good communication skills are also important when you seek professional references and letters of recommendation. I like to have confidence that my mentors and I understand one another and that what they write for or about me is of good quality.

So far, we've discussed the upper part of the "network" or "web" and how effective mentors are congruent, empathetic, useful, and focused. I have outlined several comprehensive, strong guidelines about how to qualify and seek out mentors. Now, let's examine the lower portion of the web—explaining and investigating apprentices.

As with "mentors," I do not mean "apprentice" in the traditional or historical sense (i.e., skilled trades). Rather, to me, this term means a person or friend who learns or receives advice from another. Just as the "mentor" is above, so the "apprentice" is below. In this model, the apprentice fills in the bottom section of the web or network. Again, just like with the "above" section, there can be as many nodes as desired.

Luckily for me, this model is reflexive. The network reflects itself in both directions when it comes to dual-sided social support: the things that make good mentors can also be reflected in the things that make good apprentices. For example, empathy in a mentor would be reflected by friendliness in an apprentice. Other attributes mirror one another in similar ways: positive regard is reflected by enthusiasm; congruence, by respect; and usefulness, by drive. Taking just a minute to read over that list shows how similar each one is, as well as how easily each domain overlaps and reinforces one another.

The first item in our list of desirable apprentice attributes is friendliness. Just as a mentor needs to display empathy, an apprentice needs to demonstrate friendliness. By friendliness, I mean a willingness to speak about the self and a generally happy attitude. Both of these attributes provide support for building a reciprocal relationship, one that cannot be fostered without a social connection and a match in personality. If, for example, an apprentice is gruff or uncouth, the mentor could be put off. When this is the case, learning will be much more difficult, and fostering a strong supportive relationship is nigh impossible.

Following friendliness comes enthusiasm. An apprentice needs to demonstrate a strong or genuine desire for any type of learning. In an ideal world, this enthusiasm should arise and grow continually, and in as many areas as possible. This is central for an apprentice, as that is his or her role—to learn. To nurture this enthusiasm, a mentor, as stated above, must have positive regard for his or her apprentices. This regard is a cornerstone of learning, as it fosters an apprentice's eagerness to think, grow, and realize his or her potential. Any judgment stifles this process and prevents improving the self.

Next, let's talk about respect. This is the healthy, caring respect an apprentice has for a mentor's accomplishments and experience. This is not awe or fear, but rather a general acceptance and delight derived from the mentor's skills and knowledge. Respect is important in a teaching/mentoring relationship, as it is one of the motivating factors behind the interactions in the first place. The apprentice seeks out a mentor he or she respects in order to learn about those areas in which the mentor has earned that respect. In order to build respect, mentors display competence and congruence to all potential and current apprentices. In this way, good, healthy respect is part of a two-way relationship, and it must be earned.

Lastly, let us move onto drive. This is the most difficult trait to locate and foster. By drive, I mean an overarching motivation in apprentices to improve themselves, their surroundings, or both. I say this is difficult to locate and foster because mentors cannot drag along their apprentices—the apprentices need to move themselves. This does not mean that apprentices need to do this without assistance, for mentors inherently guide and tutor those "below." Because of this, mentors must demonstrate usefulness in knowledge, skills, goals, or aspirations to their apprentices. Without this reflexive combination of drive and usefulness, the learning and tutelage will be impeded.

Again, speaking about apprentices mirrors the way we speak about mentors, so this section will look fairly similar to the earlier one on mentors, as many of the same principles apply. Just as we examined ways to find good mentors, let's look at how to find apprentices. In my experience, I've found that good apprentices can often be drawn from peers, friends, and other veterans.

Peer groups are key to success in any domain in life. This is especially true in college, as peers can provide collaborating information, areas of tutelage, advice, and suggestions for mentors or apprentices. Veterans in college normally rise above their class or peer group; I believe this is due to more life experience, increased focus and motivation, an increased ability to handle responsibility, and, in general, more social skills and stability. This provides veterans with a unique opportunity to help those budding professionals with whom they study to get a firmer grasp on life and success. Given this wealth of experience, searching for apprentices among classmates or college peers usually automatically sets a veteran above these groups. This lends itself to teaching and mentoring anyone who seems worth the time and effort, which in turn will increase social support and fulfillment.

It is also possible to draw an apprentice relationship from either short-term or long-term friends. This group is less easily defined and may overlap with the others. The easiest way to explain this is that those who already support you may also want to learn from you. Short-term or new friends may make this transition more easily than long-term friends, as a new relationship is more malleable. Here it is additionally important to watch behavior to ensure fairness and guard against an overbearing presence. In this domain, an apprenticeship is added to a friendship, rather than being metamorphosed from one into the other.

Last, and most likely easiest, the search can be done amongst other veterans, who are often searching for mentors who can teach, help, and guide them through the new, chaotic environment of college life too. As I have already explained, the transition from the military to a civilian college is difficult and confusing, and most veterans look for any friendly and non-judgmental help they can get. Veterans may have a better understanding of what they would like from a mentoring relationship, which will help it flourish. During this search, it is important to remember to speak with peers, friends, and other veterans, as opposed to a more random plan.

I have written about my thoughts, feelings, and experiences. I have written about the importance of social support as it relates to college success. I have explained my proposed theoretical model of dual-sided social support. I have even gone into detail about the different people "above" and "below" in this model. Now, one question remains: How and why does all of this work? My answer is simple: it works because of the inherent nature of military training, particularly the system and support it provides.

Historically, military training has focused on two things: critical thinking and social respect. Critical thinking refers to independent problem-solving skills designed to accomplish specific goals across a variety of changing situations. For example, everyone in the military has a clear-cut job with written responsibilities, but they also have thorough training in performing those jobs in both dangerous and mundane scenarios. This type of thinking and training creates adaptability and the goal-oriented motivation to increase leadership ability and skills. Because of the training they receive during their three to four years in the military, a vast majority of members build some measure of responsibility, both to and for other people.

These are not skills which all people possess, but they can be learned. Veterans' training and experience with critical thinking and adaptable problem-solving skills lend themselves to social success by helping veterans understand what needs to be done when interacting with a variety of people across continually changing settings. Hence, compared to their college peers, veterans are better prepared to seek out and interact more easily with both mentors and apprentices. In both of these relationships, the veteran naturally has something to learn or to teach.

Tied closely with critical and adaptable thinking is social respect. Within rank structure, social respect and etiquette are mandatory. This structure gives veterans the skills and knowledge that enables them to treat all others with respect and understanding. I must state the obvious here: social respect is a huge advantage when creating and maintaining a social support network. Combined with critical thinking skills, it can lend ease to creating and maintaining dual-sided social support. Additionally, it helps with locating and creating network relationships and nodes, and it is a set of behaviors that can be taught.

Using all of this information, a veteran can create a social support structure that is both similar to and different from military rank structure and college social circles. This distinction allows a veteran to feel accustomed to his environment while learning new or forgotten civilian social norms and habits. I think of this as a "social cushion." This cushion allows for a more gradual transition from the military to civilian life. It helps a veteran change from a strict and regimented military lifestyle to a more relaxed and self-driven college career. I truly believe that by using these methods, a veteran can achieve true success in any endeavor he or she attempts.

SHARON AGOLD
NAVY

Sharon Agold is one of the most persistent students I have ever known. As an Honors student at University of Texas at San Antonio (UTSA), she could be counted on to speak up, even when the rest of the class sat silently. Whether serving in the military, dealing with health problems, juggling family obligations, or working and going to school, she never gives up, and has the college degree to prove it.

My name is Sharon Agold. I joined the Navy when I was just seventeen years old. I was so young that my parents had to sign the enlistment documents giving their permission for me to serve. I had many reasons for wanting to join. I wanted to serve my country, earn money for college, gain experience in the world, and, perhaps most importantly, to repay a longstanding debt.

It all began when I was born two months prematurely, weighing only two pounds six ounces. My father was in the Navy at the time, so my mom delivered me at a Navy hospital. The doctors and nurses fought valiantly to save my life, and, against the odds, I survived. For that, I always felt I owed the Navy a debt, and that my service would be a way to repay that debt.

My family has been in America since before the United States became an independent nation. A member of my family has served our nation during every conflict since the Revolutionary War. As our nation began to prepare for the first Gulf War, I made my decision to join. I was not privileged to serve in the Gulf, but served stateside during that conflict. I was disappointed at first, but part of growing up is realizing that we all have to do our part. The lesson for me was that, when you volunteer to serve, you serve where you are needed. It's not about what you want, but what the Navy needs.

When my parents agreed to sign my enlistment contract, I think that my grandparents were slightly disappointed; they had hoped that I would be the first of the grandchildren to go to college. So I made a promise to them that I would go to college after I finished my enlistment. I believe that the training I went through and the experience I gained during my service were a great help to me when I finally began my college journey.

My job rating was administrative. I received training in typing, word processing, and information processing. I worked with the junior officers in my squadron, helping them prepare their yearly fitness reports. I managed the message traffic in and out of the squadron, typed and submitted the flight schedule, and issued and tracked communications gear for the planes in our squadron. I often worked under less-than-optimal conditions, including working long hours with very little sleep. These conditions were not unique to me; they occur often in squadrons and other units on deployment.

I learned many things during my service that I found helpful while I was in college. Time and stress management are at the top of the list, followed closely by leadership and study skills. Veterans and service members are respectful of authority, hardworking, and loyal. We appreciate the opportunity to go to college because we have worked so hard to get there.

I grew up a lot during my time in the Navy, and that probably made a huge difference in my grades and work ethic while I was a student. However, this is also where I encountered some difficulty. I held the expectation that the people I was taking classes with were on the same level of maturity that I was. Early on, I became frustrated when I realized that some of the students in a politics class I was taking were presenting political talking points as if they were gained first-hand through their own research. When questions of past wars and conflicts were discussed, these students were reciting memorized answers given to them by high school teachers or other college professors. They lacked any personal knowledge to back their statements.

If I had kept my concerns to myself and let my frustration fester, I might not have given the professor, or the university, a fair chance. But one lesson I learned from the military is that you have to know when to question and when to speak up for yourself, along with how to do both while showing proper respect for the authority of those in positions above you. When I brought my concerns to my professor, she took the time to explain to the class that we owed it to ourselves and our classmates to research our answers ourselves and to differentiate between facts and personal opinions when forming our answers. She also stressed respect for all viewpoints. This was a key turning point for me. I realized that the students I was having problems with weren't intentionally causing problems, and it was not right for me to assume that, just because we were in college, we were all at the same level of maturity. Our life experiences were just different.

There are things that happen in service that can cause problems for us in our personal lives and in college. Even those who never see combat face situations that most civilians will never encounter. We are given responsibilities and are asked to make decisions that affect many people. If you make a mistake in the military, it can have deleterious effects on more than just yourself and can create unimaginable stress at times.

When a military veteran starts college, the stresses and circumstances are different, but they can trigger emotions and memories that can elevate his/her stress levels and bring back strong emotions that he/she has to deal with in order to complete his/her course work. While the mistakes a student makes in college aren't potentially life-threatening, they may still produce stress, and the stress management skills veterans learn in the service come in quite handy. It can also help to find other veterans who have shared experiences and talk things through with them. During my sophomore year, I ran into a girl I went through boot camp with. We spent time talking, sharing memories, and discussing our college experiences. I don't know how beneficial that day was for her, but it was very beneficial for me.

Due to circumstances beyond my control, it took me longer than expected to graduate, but I recently received my degree in biology, with highest honors, from the Honors College at UTSA. I was finally able to keep that promise to my grandparents that I made so long ago. The perseverance that I learned beginning with my first day of basic training, and reaching all the way through my final day of service, helped make this happen. In the future I hope to study behavioral science and to conduct research into the brain and how we learn. UTSA has great professors and staff. The university is open and welcoming to veterans and active duty service members. Veterans have a great deal that we can share with our fellow students and our university; we just need to continue to do it!

NICHOLAS CARMONA
AIR FORCE

I met Nicholas Carmona while conducting research at his base, and later met with him at the University of Texas at San Antonio (UTSA) to talk about his educational goals. His joint commitment to defending his country and obtaining a college degree are even more impressive in light of his family's long history of military service and sacrifice. He is currently on active duty in South Korea.

I graduated from Stony Point High School in Round Rock, Texas in 2007. I went to Austin Community College for my freshman year and part of my sophomore year, when I left to join the service on March 10, 2009. My reasons for doing so were straightforward. Serving in the military is in my family's blood. My great-grandfather, James Albertson Cowan, served as a B-2 Flying Fortress bombardier during World War II. During a bombing mission, he was shot down and suffered shrapnel wounds from his knee to his buttocks. He went through quite a bit of rehabilitation, but I couldn't tell you the extent of his wounds or if they were permanent. As a result of his wounds, he received the Purple Heart Award, and down the road he eventually retired as a full-bird Colonel.

My grandfather, James Albertson Cowan Jr., also served in the Air Force, after graduating from Texas A&M University. He served four years and completed his career as a Captain. But that's not the end of the list: my uncle, Staff Sergeant Anthony Croff; my half-brother, Sgt. Gil Carmona III; and my non-blood brothers, Sgt. Paul River, and Spc. Philip Rivera, all served in the US Army.

When I was growing up, my friend Paul (who was practically my brother) and I loved to play with Micro Machines—toy vehicles and aircraft molded after their larger military counterparts, like the M1 Abram tank, the F-22 Raptor, the Ch-60 Blackhawk, and so forth. After the unsettling events of September 11, 2001, Paul and I vowed that one day we were going to protect our nation at all costs. In 2003, Paul enlisted in the Army. He served in Iraq as Army Infantry, and the urge to serve continued to pulsate through my veins until I took the initiative on November 8, 2008 and raised my hand to volunteer to defend my beloved nation.

Sadly, Paul was killed in action in Afghanistan in 2011. This had a significant impact on my life because Paul was like a mentor to me. When my biological father would leave me sitting by a windowsill, Paul would come over and turn my day around. He built me up into the man I am today, teaching me to care about those around me and to help them whenever the opportunity arises. I know when I have a wife and children one day I won't do what my father did to me. The loss of Paul did put stress on everyone in my family, especially since he was a key part of our lives. His parents and family were devastated, but over time the scar has healed, although his physical presence here on earth is dearly missed.

I am currently in the Air Force and have been stationed at Joint Base San Antonio-Lackland Air Force Base, Texas, for the past four and a half years. My current duty title is installation patrolman; I am also armory certified to distribute weapons and ammo to Security Forces personnel who are arming to protect the base. From July 15, 2010 to January 31, 2011, I was based at Joint Base Balad, Iraq, where I was a part of Operations Iraqi Freedom and New Dawn. My second deployment was to King Faisal Air Base, Jordan, as part of Operation Eager Lion in 2012. My current rank is Senior Airman.

Before joining the military, I knew I wanted to go to college, and I have since completed my associate's Degree in Criminal Justice from Community College Air Force. I have also been attending the American Military University, but have put it on hold to attend Airman Leadership School. This noncommissioned officer school will allow me to become a frontline supervisor. Last October (three days after a close friend of mine committed suicide), I was sent to Military Working Dog Handlers Course (MWD for short), and on January 16th of this year, I graduated, and now I handle a four-legged friend.

This is some of the best training I have ever received, just because I get to work around dogs every day. But I'm not going to lie; these dogs not only have agility, they also have one hell of a bite. Some of the brute power they force upon a fleeing individual will definitely make one think before running from the police, but if you learn certain techniques, like I did, you can trick a dog during a pursuit. This helps to train the dog so that if it encounters such tricks, it can make a quick decision about how to handle that particular incident. Unfortunately, after I graduated, I received orders to PCS (permanent change of station) to Minot AFB, North Dakota. I had developed a minor sleeping disorder after Iraq, and the commander didn't see me as "suitable for that type of working environment."

Immediately following that disapproval, I met up with the Chief of my Security Forces Squadron, Chief Master Sergeant Fuller, who sat me down one day and asked about how long I had been on station. When I told him that I wanted to "progress my career" by going to a new base, he agreed with me and asked me where I wanted to go in particular. Without hesitation, I spurted out "Korea!" "Are you sure? If you are absolutely positive, I can make it happen!" Chief told me. I nodded my head and confirmed it with a "yes" answer.

Not more than two weeks later, I received an e-mail from AFPC (Air Force Personnel Center) stating that I had a new assignment. Sure enough, I got Korea, and on the fifth of January, 2015, I arrived at Osan AB, Republic of Korea (ROK), to being a new adventure in life. This first Permanent Change of Station (PCS) will be beneficial in the long-term for my career. Being stationed at one base for your entire career wouldn't be beneficial (other than getting to know quite a few people). Staying in one place for long periods of time can hinder your career, especially in the Air Force; however, if you apply yourself in different positions throughout your career field, that's definitely a plus. Being a new handler, I needed to get more experience in the field, and since they do large-scale exercises in Korea, I can get to experience this type of atmosphere, one unlike what we would receive in the states. Getting used to a jungle, farmland environment was an eye-opening experience, but when it gets cold—and yes, it does get extremely cold—you will freeze, even with multiple layers on (you will sweat because of the cold and then that sweat will freeze up).

I was assigned a dog right from the start of my PCS. Her name is Emmra, a seven-year-old Belgian Malinois that was on point with her work ethic, but during training one day she sustained an injury that put her out of commission for quite some time. After completing a combat readiness course, my unit was in need of more handlers on flight and thus got me a new dog. His name is Bivoly/N706. He is a pure black German Shepard, and as of July 6, 2015, he turned seven years old. From the get-go, Biv and I bonded incredibly quickly, and within in a week we were validated as a working dog team and sent to days flight. Over the course of almost a year, we located many things around base, which in turn made us stand out amongst other handlers. I don't go above the call of duty, but I will outperform and work my tail off to do what needs to be accomplished. I also take the time to improve Biv and myself as a team so we can be much more proficient.

Coming over here, I had written out tons of goals, such as getting the highest score possible on my yearly performance report, which I did. I also passed my on-duty job qualifications with very high scores (one of which was 100) and passed the promotions test. I put on my new rank ten days after I was selected, and now I am a Staff Sergeant in the United States Air Force! I took four college courses and passed all with 90s and above, and now I'm about to take my career development course test; I have confidence I will pass it, just like everything else I have passed, making this year that much more successful.

I have made incredible friends and bonds that can't be broken. I have learned who my true friends are, and I know those who, if I departed, would show that they never really cared. Osan has truly been a blessing in disguise, but I am ready to get to my new base, Dyess AFB in Abilene, Texas, to start my next adventure in the Air Force. I look forward to being the best Military Working Dog Handler and Patrol Officer I can be; also, I should be graduating with my BA as well, and possibly moving on to a Masters.

I will be here for a year, and after that I will have a follow-on assignment of my choice. I put down Germany, UK, Alaska, and Hawaii. Personally, I want Germany so I can travel all over Europe. I would especially like to go to the Holocaust locations and many key battlegrounds from World War II.

Before I knew I was going to have to move again, I applied to UTSA because it was located near my base. I was very surprised when I was accepted, because I have never applied to a big name college before. I felt overwhelming joy and pride when I saw the acceptance letter. It wasn't an easy process, though. Of the eighty-five college credits I have accumulated from previous institutions, only forty were accepted towards my four-year degree. Given the fact that I had to attend multiple schools because of my service, I think all of the credit hours I previously earned should be applied to my degree.

However, in spite of that minor glitch, I have appreciated the support I've gotten from the admissions staff at UTSA. While being in the military didn't really influence me to go to college, it did help me to develop a "never quit" attitude. In my opinion, studying for a difficult class is still far easier than trying to sleep through a barrage of bombs, and finding my way around a college campus is easier than arguing with a foreign national!

I picked my major, criminal justice, because it coincides with my passion for law enforcement. In my heart and soul I believe I have the integrity to uphold the law and keep our country safe. It's not that I want to wear a gun to look cool. Rather, I have the drive to protect others, and I am not afraid to put my life on the line, even for someone I don't know. This is something that was definitely influenced by what my "brother," Paul, did for me and the ultimate sacrifice he made that tragic day in October, 2011, but I have also always had this type of mindset—putting others first before myself.

My future goals are to finish my undergraduate degree and, hopefully, to be hired by the Secret Service or a federal law enforcement agency. Along the way, I hope to help my mom turn her passion for baking cakes into a successful, full-time business. My last goal is kind of cheesy, but I would like to find the gal of my dreams and raise a family out in the country. Something about the country is implanted in my mind, and I would like to wake up every morning to the rising sun and sit on the porch every evening to watch the sunset with her.

I can tell you one thing being about being a soldier and veteran: we are the most outspoken, professional individuals you will ever meet. When it comes to asking questions, taking the initiative, showing up in class fifteen minutes prior to the start of class, or staying after to finish the assignment, we go the extra mile. Younger students who go to college straight out of high school don't tend to have the same work ethic and ability to handle life's challenges when duty calls. I believe that my military service has prepared me to pick up a rifle, to earn a college degree, or to do whatever else is needed to help my country.

BRIAN HOUSTON
NAVY

Brian Houston is an energetic, confident young man who volunteered to become a member of my Veteran Scholars Research Group the minute he heard about it. It is this sort of willingness to step up and make things happen that characterizes both his military and academic careers.

I am a veteran. I earned this title through four years of service to the U.S. Navy. When I left for the service, I had burnt all my bridges at home and had nowhere to go. I had just barely finished high school, and never really thought much about college. The first branch I wanted to go into was the Army, on a buddy plan with my best friend, but since I had made some prior bad choices, he ended up going alone. In the meantime, my mother talked to a Navy recruiter, who contacted me and kept telling me how the women of the world loved the Navy uniform, like that had some magic meaning that I longed for. I had never really thought much about the Navy, since I wanted to shoot guns and go to war (my sense of patriotism was so strong). I also had a sense of pride about the Army; my father was in the Army (as was his father), but his twin brother and stepfather were in the Navy, and several of my cousins are in the Air Force.

You can imagine the conversations that occurred when my father heard I was going into the Navy. I was a traitor. But I had hope for a better life and a way out of the stalled position I found myself in. When I sat in my recruiter's office, I realized I really had no one to say goodbye to, and that I also had no choice. It was more of a good-riddance situation. Prior to that, I had driven a family heirloom into a house; a family member was furious, and while he was driving me to the recruiter, I asked if I could get my phone to say my last goodbyes. Nope. The family member took me over to the mall and said to the entire recruiting office, "Here, you take him."

The moment I realized there was no turning back was at the airport in Chicago. Boot camp was "just down the street," where a huge group of young people were sleeping and chatting, thinking they knew what was about to happen.

When I joined, I had less than $200. I had been unemployed for months, I was skipping from house to house, and I was on the fast track to prison. I was reckless, and I had no aspirations of ever making it past the age of twenty-three. Of course, time plays its role and things often pan out, and life became simple and stable for me, which was nice for a change. I had a place to stay, new beginnings, a nice steady paycheck, and no bills. Good times were definitely had. I worked out constantly and remained healthy.

In the Navy, my first paycheck went directly to pay for my uniforms in boot camp, but the next one gave me my first taste of the amazing feeling that comes with financial stability. The first few checks after that made me feel just as good. Some people complained about the money, but I thought they just weren't good at keeping their finances together. Although I went shopping and brought my friends along most of the time, I also learned the value of saving money. I figured out how to create and stick to a budget. My only bill was me and my taste for guitars.

At first, I thought four years was going to be short—I would serve my time and get out. I wouldn't mess with anyone, and I would stick to my own. Of course, that didn't happen, because there was usually someone who was prone to mess with you or talk trash to you, and since I'm a talker, it seemed unusual to not speak. But with the multiple groups, subgroups, and cliques in the Navy, I found myself gathering around people who had similar interests, humor, and lifestyle. Assimilation begins with this innate feeling of needing to belong.

My job in the Navy was very similar to that of a supply warehouse worker. Shipments came and went. Sometimes nothing would happen, and sometimes the action would be nonstop, lasting a few days. Although work performance and efficiency are the direct responsibility of the people at the lowest level of the chain, morale and liberty were handed out by those at the higher end of the ranking ladder. It was a very micro-managed setting, and attention to detail was crucial.

Of course, when you hear Navy, you automatically associate it with travel. I have been to Dubai, Japan, Thailand, Singapore, Hong Kong, and Hawaii. Deployments were very different from what I had imagined. Although some stops were longer in duration than others, I discovered that everywhere I went, each place had a very different, rich culture and history. I made it a point to get lost and go far away from wherever our ship had pulled in. I went into the local area to explore the culture. I felt like I was on a mission to use my senses to the fullest, and to gain as much knowledge as I could from the people I met there. It opened my eyes and humbled me. It sowed a deep love for my country and a commitment to strive hard and climb the capitalistic ladder, because we, unlike the people of many countries, have the chance to do so.

Being out to sea for long periods of time is a tough experience. While some people love and live for it, there are others who hate and fear it. I enjoyed the benefits of travel, but I also feared the dangers of a sinking ship. I disliked the repetitive cycle of daily chores, jokes, fights, orders, and training. I found it frustrating when a stranger walked over a freshly mopped floor with their oil-splattered, dirty boots, because I knew I was going to have to mop or strip and wax it again and again—and I'd probably have to do it the next day, too.

Things got repetitive during downtime as well. We told stories until we ran out of ones we hadn't heard already. We played the same games and tried hard not to watch the same movies or read the same books. I also found that my mind created an abnormal longing to see trees and grass, dogs and kids, mountains and buildings. Because I worked nights, I went for weeks with no sun, living like a worm in the bottom soil of a rusty pot. Sometimes it felt as if I was living alone, even though I was surrounded by hundreds of people every day.

Being in the Navy makes relationships difficult. Some of my shipmates had significant others, but my problem was finding one. As soon as a lady heard that I was in the Navy, she didn't want me anymore. It's easy to understand why: I was gone every two weeks, for two or three weeks at a time. Being in a relationship with someone in the military is a lifestyle many people can't handle.

Beyond the everyday difficulties of serving on the ship, sailors are affected by global events that are out of their control. There are times when your emotions are more dominant than your cognitive reasoning. But when the situation is out of anyone's control, we have to accept it as a bad experience and carry on. During wartime, training never ends because we have to be ready to respond rapidly and intuitively. There are rules of war that we must follow. We must trust the process. The bad side is that other countries don't necessarily care to follow these rules. This at times puts us in danger.

The adherence to rules prevents barbarism, but it also sometimes prevents safety. I worked at night, and was assigned to a gun mounted to the side of the ship. One night, an Iranian Coast Guard boat came about, very close to our ship. It was so close I couldn't even point the gun down towards it because we were placed so far on the overhang. Thoughts of the USS Cole were running through my head. The boat flashed its lights at us, rode next to us less than ten feet away along the entire length of the ship, then disappeared into the darkness.

In addition to the horrors of war, family crises can take their toll. When there's a death in the family and you're in a no-fly zone, you can't make it back. When your loved ones need to reach you, the e-mail on the ship might go down. All these things make you feel helpless—and you are.

A downside of military training is that it may not make you qualified to do the same job back in civilian society. For example, if you are an electrician in the military, that experience doesn't qualify you to do electrical work in a home. The service does allow journeymen's or apprenticeship hours to be completed, but if, for instance, you want to be an aircraft parts machinist, you will have to get certified or trained professionally in the public sector. You also better hope your higher up will grant you the time.

With all this being said, I would like to lighten up a little by sharing my academic experiences. After I left the military, I was determined to continue on to school. When I took those first few steps on my first college campus, I had a feeling of enlightenment and accomplishment. I never ever expected to be there, and I was excited to be taking advantage of a benefit I received because of my service. It felt so good, I was smiling the whole first day.

Of course, I did have initial anxieties: What are they going to think of my age? How can I do this when I've been "turning a wrench" for the last four years? Are these just kids here? I read very slowly, and I couldn't type. My handwriting was, and still is, horrible. I didn't develop good study habits. Because of all these worries, I doubted myself and forecast my own failure, and my work suffered in the first year of school. What saved me from giving up? My curiosity, my interest in the subject matter, and the fact that I am highly motivated by fear of failure.

By the second year, I had gotten over the social anxieties. In fact, by then I was becoming too social, and that in itself was turning into a problem, so I had to reassess my goals and motivational drives. I learned that each teacher has his or her own style, and that they will gladly share the goals of the class with you. I've developed useful study techniques. If you study for each class one extra hour or go over the past material more than once, information is so much more easily retained. Reading the textbook chapters twice also helps me, as does doing additional outside research on YouTube. Getting together with classmates to study helps because other students speak on the same educational level as I do.

I received my associate's degree at a college in Washington State. That moment was just the same as high school graduation: I finished, and then moved. I sold all of my furniture to make it down to Texas, where I am currently studying at UTSA. I graduated with a BA in psychology, but my thirst for more has not been satisfied. I am now in a graduate study program. While at UTSA, I have taken every opportunity to enhance my educational experiences.

The service definitely picked me up out of the rut I was in. It taught me to be a man, how to take care of things, and to ask for help when it is needed. I would never have achieved higher education if not for the Navy. Education is something I highly value. I thank every service person I see for their sacrifice. I know what I've gained and what others can gain. It's an experience, that's for sure. It just depends on the person to make it as valuable as possible.

WILL HARRIS
NAVY

Will is the sort of student who was apologetic about missing class, despite the fact that it occurred because he was hospitalized with a serious infection. Whether working to support his mom and his siblings or salvaging plane parts after accidents, Will has an abiding interest in understanding leadership from both a personal and a psychological perspective.

I joined the service because my family and I were struggling to keep a roof over our heads and food on the table. I have five younger sisters (the oldest of whom is mentally disabled) and an older half-brother who was in prison at the time I joined.

My dad left around the time I was twelve. He is back now, trying to help out when he can, but he was gone until about the time I left to join the military. He is a retired Vietnam veteran and engineer. When he was living with us, he worked at Kelly Air Force Base fixing plane engines. Sometimes I would go watch him run up engines. I thought it was awesome, which is why I decided to work on jets when I joined the Navy.

In high school, I played football—which kept me sane—and I worked part-time jobs. In fact, I had worked part-time jobs since grade school, giving all that money to my mom. In addition to mowing lawns, I worked in an antique restoration store, as a church janitor, and at just about all the well-known fast food restaurants. I worked in construction, as a window panel installer, as a member of hotel cleanup staff, as a telemarketer, as a door-to-door phone salesman, and even more. While all that was going on, my Mom had her own ice cream truck business. So every weekend after mowing lawns, I would be the "ice cream man." Until high school, that's what all the kids at school called me. During the winter, we would change it to a taco stand and go to construction sites.

I wanted to do a lot of things when I graduated from high school. I wanted to travel the world and play football at a college. But none of it was going to happen. Unfortunately, my family and I were still going through hard times. My mom wasn't able to keep up with the bills for the house, gas, and food for me and my sisters, even with my help. Also at that time, my youngest sister had to have surgery on her leg, which put her in a wheelchair for quite some time and kept my mom from going to work sometimes. After high school, I ended up becoming a full-time manager at a Whataburger.

I started thinking about going into the military when 9/11 happened. After watching the coverage on television that day, I wanted to join the fight against terrorism. I went to a naval recruitment center, which was right down the street, and asked them what they had to offer. When they said I could work on planes, travel the world, get a big sign-up bonus, receive GI Bill benefits, and earn a monthly paycheck almost twice as much as I was getting paid currently, I was sold. I could send some money home to help my mom, and would be able to do some of the other things I wanted to accomplish.

While I did get to do some of those things, there were other experiences I wasn't counting on. Once I had to search the wreckage of an aircraft that contained the body parts of a pilot I had worked with on a daily basis. Before flight, he and I would walk around the jet to make sure that all of our concerns were addressed. When that was done, I would launch him out (which involved strapping him into his seat) and signal him when to start, testing and revving his engines. While this was going on, I was also responsible for the safety of the people who were working on and around the jet as it was started up and while it was running.

Fortunately, I was not the plane captain for his last flight, because I don't know how I would have dealt with that type of burden. When I was searching the wreck, I kept thinking about how the plane captain (someone I knew well too) was thinking and feeling at the time. To complicate things further, the emergency reclamation team I was part of is typically only responsible for reclaiming the wreckage and the black box. There is another team that is supposed to be there for body reclamation, but that day we did it.

Another time I was on a ship working night ops when the plane captain next to me was blown into the path of his jet by the exhaust form another jet. The pilot is on the left-front side of the jet, just aft of the nose of the aircraft, and its temperature gets up past two thousand degrees. The whole side of the captain's face melted off in front me, and I saw his blood splatter all over the place. I could not leave my jet to help—you're ordered not to leave your jet no matter what happens. I could only signal for help.

Fortunately, I have also had plenty of other not-so-grim experiences, like when I was sent TAD (Temporary Additional Duty) for two weeks to the galley, and had the chance to burn over two thousand cookies and fifty pies in one day. Needless to say, not many people enjoyed dessert that day.

My transition from the military to the university was a complete headache, to say the least. I had just completed a deployment when I found out that someone had broken into my apartment and stolen a checkbook. They had written checks the whole time I was on deployment—over $10,000 worth—so I had to fix that. Two weeks later, I was honorably discharged and went home. A week later my new apartment was also broken into, and just a week later I was in school. So, while taking my first classes, I had to deal with both the insurance company and all the paperwork to get my GI Bill benefits going. That was a nightmare.

I was planning to talk about the difficulties I had with actually doing the work and knowing where to get the help if I needed it, but I haven't had time to do that.

2

LIFE AFTER SEPARATION

BONNIE DRUSKY
AIR FORCE

Bonnie is one of the students who sits near the front of the class, nods enthusiastically when she hears something that interests her, and never hesitates to speak up in class. Her enthusiasm for learning and optimistic outlook on life are particularly impressive in light of the obstacles she has already had to overcome in her life. I suspect that many of her classmates are surprised when she mentions that she was in the military, but she quickly engages them with her infectious laugh and intriguing stories.

I was born in New Orleans Charity Hospital on July 21, 1988. My mother and father both had military connections in their lives. My father was from a Pennsylvania family with four boys who all joined different branches of military service. My mother was, according to her birth certificate, a "military brat," born in Georgia to an Army private and his wife. Both of my parents had many financial hardships that were furthered by addiction to alcohol and battles with depression.

Shortly after I was born, my mother's ongoing alcoholism became so severe that she could no longer walk, and she passed away in her sleep when I was three years old. My father was in his sixties, but despite his age, he did the best he could to raise me. He would go so far as to ask my godmother to babysit me, and often neighbors did their part to try to feed me for free.

His story is one I hardly know because alcoholism and depression took a great toll on his ability to take an active positive role in my life. The few memories I have of him are of his stories about the military and his hopes that one day I would become a teacher. I found it hard to continue to live with him, as I was at times raising myself, so I went to my priest, who took it upon himself to have the local religious school catechism director take me into foster care. Two years later, a heart attack ended my father's life.

I lived with my foster family for eight years as a homeschooled young lady who often took trips to art museums, plantations, and fine restaurants. I was raised to know about the different cultures and religions of the world. I took an interest in studying the basics of American Sign Language, Ancient Egyptian history, and various religions around the globe. I spent many Sundays, after attending church service as an altar server, engaging in debates with my older foster sister and learning to cook from my Sicilian foster grandmother.

My time with Father Kenneth and my foster mother was filled with many intellectual conversations that included religion. I had actually considered the idea of becoming a nun because I felt at peace when I was discussing God, but I soon realized that I had too much spunk to be a nun. I spent so much time in conversation with priests about their homilies that I felt more of a connection to the priesthood than the convent. Since priesthood is solely a male role in the Catholic Church, I searched for a different path for my life.

It wasn't long after Hurricane Katrina had forced my foster family and me to move to Texas that I was told that it was time for me to figure out what I wanted to do with my life. This was due to the fact that after I turned eighteen, the government would no longer provide assistance to support my living with my foster family. I had to figure where to go because staying in the home with my foster family would place a financial burden on them.

After many weeks of painstaking consideration, I still wasn't sure what I wanted to do with my life, since staying home and going to college was not an option. My foster family suggested that I join the Job Corps of America and take up a trade, but I wasn't sure what trade I would take, and I knew that I wanted to travel. I soon realized that the answer was right in front of me: I had spent my entire teenage life watching news coverage of the war in Iraq, and I realized that if my father and my grandfather could join the military, I knew I had it in me to follow in their footsteps.

The year of my high school graduation, I enlisted in the United States Air Force in Houston, Texas. My foster family had mixed feelings about my decision to join the military. They were concerned that I was putting myself into a war, and they were afraid for my safety. My answer was that if I waited to join in a few years when the war might end, who is to say another war won't begin? I felt that it was better to go and take a position in the military then than to wait. I also knew that it was far better for me take some form of action as a symbol for a change than to be on my knees praying for the world to resolve itself.

In a matter of weeks into basic training, I was given a job as a services mission support troop. It was the best thing that could be given to me within such short notice of my signing up, with no time to wait for a particular job opening to become available. I was pleased that I was a noncombatant troop whose main focus was to help tend to the needs of soldiers in a caregiving role. I enjoyed learning to cook, basic fitness, lodging with accountability of troops, and the basics of setting up a tentative war base.

I joined the Air Force with the intention of learning leadership skills, traveling, and attending college. During my time in service, I learned to expect change, to be open about plans and strategies, to pay attention and listen to others, and to be ready for anything. I was an Airman First Class in the Force Support Readiness career field, whose main focus is on tending to the needs of other airmen—making sure their basic needs are met, whether we are on base or in a war zone. I found this to be a position I was well suited for, although I did find it challenging at times, since the majority of my time at work was with other troops in a kitchen working to feed hundreds of people at home base. I did have to train with a weapon, but I was never expected to actually have to shoot outside the firing range.

My time in Iraq was spent at Sather AFB. I worked as a lodging troop with duties that varied from cleaning and reporting accountability of the number of people on base to PERSCO, to creating games and events for the troops. Regardless of whether I was at home station or in Iraq, my job was customer service in nature; therefore, the troops spent a great deal of time chatting with me, almost as if I were their bartender. Some of them would tell me about their day at work, how they were coping with being overseas, the awards they received, or the various fun things they were doing when they took leave.

In England, the most thrilling part of the cook position was that my "weekends" were given during weekdays. Whenever I could, I would report to one of my supervisors that I was going on a day trip to London. I would book a taxi to the train station and then hop a ride into the city. I purposefully would not bring a map with me—I wanted to get lost in the history and the shops around me.

During one visit to London, I got lost after getting my hair done at a spa. I found myself wandering around in a park that looked as if it were a huge university area. I walked around, taking in the beauty of the green, lush grass under the blanket of gray sky that can only be recreated by an artist who's been in England. I enjoyed the view of the ducks wandering around, the people reading on blankets with their children. I felt as if I was privileged to be at a private show of life.

I had spent the day walking past Big Ben and finding English food along the way. These were all the delightful experiences of English history that I always hoped for, but I discovered that walking around in the park on an ordinary day in England was far more enjoyable. This park was completely free of charge and as beautiful as any painting in an art museum. For the rest of my three-year stay in England, I made a note to visit each city that I could in order to take in at least one historical landmark, followed by finding a way to get lost.

After I was honorably discharged from the service as a result of a medical issue, I moved back to Texas, but I had no one to depend on. I was glad to come back to San Antonio, since it is where I did my military basic training, and I knew that it was a place that had a rich culture filled with southern charms, similar to New Orleans. Fortunately, the GI Bill and the Vocation Rehabilitation Program made college attainable for me. In addition, since I had joined the military as a resident of Texas, I was eligible for the Hazelwood Act, which pays the tuition for a post-graduate degree. Even though the military was the only job I ever had, I decided to go to college and find a job. After months of paperwork, medical appointments, moving, and unemployment, I began college at the age of twenty-two.

I started my studies at San Antonio Community College, with the goal of transferring to the University of Texas at San Antonio. Because of my military experience, I felt I had a sense of worldliness and maturity that other students lacked. In the beginning, I found it difficult to balance finding work and transportation, furnishing an apartment, and creating a class schedule.

Fortunately, I knew that I wasn't alone in searching to find a sense of belonging after service. I chose an academic advisor at San Antonio College who was a UTSA alumni veteran to be my mentor. He guided me through the process of studying whatever my heart was willing to learn. I started college feeling that I couldn't hold my own in any classroom because I needed remedial math classes, which set back my academic graduation date. However, I was taking college-level English classes because my advisor had faith in my ability to retake and pass the entrance exams for those courses. I spent nearly every semester reporting my grades (which were mostly high) to him, as well as giving him the play-by-play of my next semester lineup. In the spring of 2014, I graduated from San Antonio with an associate's degree in Psychology and American Sign Language.

During the last two years of my associate's degree, my biological sister came back into my life after a long separation. She listened to me speak of the fun of getting school supplies and how excited I was to have a "five jalapeño"-rated professor for the following semester. She also encouraged me to continue to push through the difficult exams, reminding me that it would be all worth it in the end. She was there on the phone with me when I received my acceptance letter to UTSA. I am the first of my father's line to attend college and to go on for a bachelor's degree. She told me she was proud that I am the first of my father's line to attend college and go on for a bachelor's degree, and that my father would be proud of me as well. Unfortunately, she passed away unexpectedly after the first day I attended UTSA.

My fascination with making connections with people and exploring the way they behave has always held a place in my heart, and it became apparent to me that learning more about how people operate was a calling I needed to fulfill. This led me to continue the expansion of my associate's degree in Psychology at UTSA.

Being on campus at UTSA felt similar to my overseas experience. I found it was more important than ever to immerse myself in the crowd of people at campus and to keep pushing forward for the sake of the experience of university life, no matter the grades. I had ample opportunity to learn more about local art and foods through events held on campus. I found the atmosphere to be just as inviting as the community college; the staff was as approachable and inviting as I could hope for.

In addition, the diversity of the student population and the professors on the UTSA campus afforded me the opportunity outside the classroom to make use of the basic Arabic and art history that I learned. As outgoing as I am, I've enjoyed the chance to talk with professors from various fields of study about classes I had undertaken or debates about recent history.

More importantly, through talking to other veterans and forming study groups, I realized that I was not alone on campus. I discovered that many other veterans were trying to balance whole new identities as students. We all believed that higher education would make our lives better, and the American Dream is very much alive in the hearts of veteran college students. This eased my feeling of disconnect when speaking up in class about my view of the world.

With the help of Ms. Wendy Foster, who also has a background in psychology and American Sign Language, I switched from being on the GI Bill to using the vocational rehabilitation program benefits. I told her of my anxiety about the process, and she was very kind and considerate to help me with the process of continuing my education. At times, just running into her in the hallway gave me a reason to chat and to have someone else to look up to and to make proud of any small achievement that I could.

Since I wasn't the typical age of a student, I felt somewhat shy about interacting with anyone other than the professor in the classroom. I generally sat in the front of the class to assure that

I was focused, but also to keep the sense of it being just myself and the professor, just like when I was homeschooled. Soon after I got to UTSA, the Student Veterans Club, which had many students from San Antonio College who transferred to UTSA, started inviting me to various gatherings that offered information on job fairs for veterans. I also found that, because I was so outgoing in class, other students frequently wanted to talk to me when they saw me in the library or the hallway.

I took Psychology of Stress in the summer of 2014, where I became friends with a fellow student named Jordan. He became like a brother to me because he was also adopted and a non-traditional student. The professor for the class was very kind and good at showing us that stress is often a product of how we choose to react to situations that happen in our lives. I learned from her class that my anxiety as a student is often a result of having unrealistic expectations and not doing what I can in the present.

I realized that being good with people was a skill that I broadened through the military. I may not have felt I was the best student, but I could speak up in class. I found that to learn meant not always being right (and that was perfectly fine), but more so that the humility of saying "I don't know" was a skill I could use to help other students become more comfortable in the classroom. Often when students notice my outgoing personality, they welcome creating study groups together.

I essentially learned that, at times, it isn't the skill but the desire to learn that can lead to the greatest progress. Through my interactions with students, people I've come to know in the Veteran's Administration Office, and with professors in the classroom, I found that anyone could be a mentor and inspire confidence in others. I learned that in order to succeed, everyone needs to belong and to have a sense of purpose.

MELANIE MOSER
AIR FORCE

Melanie once wrote a twenty-page research paper for me as part of an Independent Study project. While this might be a daunting task for many students, Melanie completed the project, from her mother's house, while recovering from major back surgery. She has since completed a graduate degree in mental health counseling and guidance.

In high school, I was in Air Force ROTC. It was the first place I felt like I was really part of something. I was truly convinced the Air Force was going to be the path I chose for my life, but after graduation, I was less sure of where I was going. By the age of twenty-two, I felt like my life had no purpose. I had dropped out of college twice, and was going from one menial job to another. I'm not sure why, but I had never gone to see a recruiter to enlist. At least in part, it was because I knew that in order to serve I would have to hide who I was. The "Don't Ask, Don't Tell" policy was still in place, so I was very scared that if I tried to serve and my sexuality was discovered, I would be dismissed from service. I ended up putting the thought and desire to enlist out of my mind.

On September 10, 2001, I was fired from a well-known company for being gay. In Texas, anyone can be fired without cause or reason. They call it "at will employment." I was frustrated, living with my parents, and had no direction. I woke up on the morning of September 11, 2001 to the horror on our television. I sat and watched as our beautiful country was attacked. I was glued to the coverage, much like every other American. I watched as the smoke billowed from the North Tower of the World Trade Center in New York after being hit by American Airlines Flight 11. I watched as United Airlines Flight 175 impacted the South Tower of the World Trade Center in New York. I watched as thousands ran across the Pentagon's green lawn after American Airlines Flight 77 hit the western side of the building. I learned of the heroic story of the passengers on United Airlines Flight 93 who attempted to gain back control of the plane. Sadly, those brave people failed to regain control of the aircraft, but they did succeed in preventing the plane from hitting another building. On each of those four flights, all lives were lost. Our country was devastated. Many had perished, and many were left injured. By the end of the day I was left with an overwhelming desire to do something to help.

The next morning, I drove to the blood bank and stood in line all day to donate blood. Once I was done, I did not feel like I had done enough. I knew there was only one way I could fill this need inside of me to do my part. On September 13, 2001, I went straight to an Air Force recruiter and began the paperwork to enlist. I somehow knew this was the correct decision.

Due to the influx of people enlisting post-9/11, I was placed on delayed enlistment. It was not until April 16, 2002, the day after my twenty-third birthday, that I was able to leave for basic training. The day I was sworn in was the best day of my life, yet I knew I had to put part of who I was on a shelf. I was comfortable with that; I was going to be a soldier and help defend my country.

Since Air Force basic training was in my hometown of San Antonio, Texas, I was permitted to be dropped off by my mother. This ultimately made for a very emotional goodbye and a very difficult first day of basic training. Certainly, in basic training they wasted no time getting in our faces and instilling the fear of God in each one of us. The first week seemed like a bad dream.

We had no uniforms, and all we did was march in the hot sun and study the books we had been given. The day we were issued our uniforms was the day I truly felt like a soldier. It was a very proud moment for me. We were no longer dressed in our civilian clothes; we were all in the same uniform. We were one unit, ready to do what we needed for our country. By the end of basic training, I was a very different person. I walked proudly with my head held high; I was a soldier. I was A1C Moser.

I was quickly shipped off to technical school in Wichita, Texas. It was far from the most luxurious place to be, but I was glad to be out of basic training and ready to begin my Air Force education. I was scheduled to become a medical technician, but I soon discovered that I had broken my foot during basic training. The pain had been worsening progressively since I had left basic training, and I was finally instructed to see a doctor, who ran x-rays and placed me in a walking boot. They did not want to perform any type of surgery on that training base, so my job was changed to medical administration. This involved a shorter training period and allowed me to arrive back at my home base, Lackland Air Force Base in San Antonio.

I successfully completed my training in three months, but what I did not know was how much more damage I had done walking on a broken foot for three months. I had caused permanent damage to both the nerves and the broken bone. I was devastated. Had I ended my career before it had even begun?

I loved my unit, the 433rd Aeromedical Staging Squadron. The people were great, and functioned as a cohesive unit. There was always talk of deployment overseas, but the orders had not come. We were placed on standby a couple of times, but nothing ever developed. I was glad at the time that we were not shipped out, because I was on medical hold, continuing to have medical tests to determine the extent of the damage to my foot. Eventually I had surgery.

Although I was anxious to recover and return to my unit, things did not go as planned. The nerve damage was too extensive, and my foot would never be the same. After only two short years in the United States Air Force, I was given an Honorable Medical Discharge in May of 2004. I was no longer who I had wanted to be. I had not done anything to help my country. I was lost. I began drinking every day and became very depressed. Once again, my life had no direction and I felt like a failure.

I began receiving treatment with Dr. Celeste Borchers at Audie L. Murphy VA Hospital Podiatry Clinic. She ultimately decided to perform yet another surgery on my foot, this time to release a trapped nerve that was causing me a great deal of pain. She was able to release the nerve, but too much damage had already been done, and the nerve was partially dead. I am very grateful to Dr. Borchers, regardless of the pain I was still experiencing. She was able to decrease the pain some and allow me more mobility than I previously had. At that point I truly realized that I would never be the same physically.

At this point, although I still didn't know what I wanted to do, my family urged me to return to school. I learned of a program to become a respiratory therapist, and once again felt that I had a purpose. But, with constant pain and only one semester left, I was forced to drop out to have surgery once again. The pain in my foot was so bad that I had a spinal cord stimulator implanted. I was sure this would give me the relief I needed to continue with my education, but, sadly, it did not. It only caused more problems, except now they were in my back. I was becoming a mess. My doctors informed me that it would not be in my best interest to finish my degree in respiratory therapy. Once again, I was lost, with no direction, and I relapsed back into depression.

While I was receiving medical care at the VA, the doctors noticed my depressed state and referred me for mental health care. I was fortunate enough to work for about six years with a psychologist who never let me give up. She saw something in me that even I didn't see. She helped guide me to places I didn't know existed and find strength in myself I didn't know I had. I was able to receive money from the VA to attend school. It is because of her that I chose to study psychology.

I was able to finish my bachelor's degree at UTSA in a year and a half, but I had no idea where I'd go from there. Although the university didn't provide much specific counseling for veterans, I did receive guidance and support from a few select professors. While the transition from community college to a university was far from easy, these professors made it bearable and, eventually, comfortable. There was so many days that I did not think I would ever amount to anything, but I did end up completing my undergraduate degree.

I have now completed a graduate degree in mental health counseling and guidance. My goal is to work for the VA or a military facility and give back to the soldiers and veterans who were able to fight for our country. I want to be able to give them the guidance and hope I was given. My path was never easy, and there were many times I felt like giving up, but it all led to where I am supposed to be. I will still be able to help our country and our heroes, just not in the way I had originally thought.

I am eternally grateful for the many people who helped me get to this place in my life. My family, specifically my mother, was a constant support system through all my trials, and never once gave up on me. My best friend, Jennifer, walked by my side and never stopped encouraging me to be better than I was the day before. My mental health provider never let me quit and showed me just how much life had to offer.

I would also like to thank a few of my professors for their support, understanding, and guidance: Dr. Anthony Scott (Psychology Department at UTSA), Dr. Terri Earnest (Sociology Department at UTSA), and last but, definitely not least, Dr. Mary McNaughton-Cassill, also with the Psychology Department at UTSA. Thank you, Dr. McNaughton-Cassill, for being so supportive and caring so deeply for our nation's veterans.

JOAN JOHNSON
ARMY SPOUSE

Joan is both a "military brat" and two-time military spouse who managed to raise a family despite moving all over the country. While all of that moving didn't make it easy for her to finish college, it certainly taught her how to manage stress. She was a student in several of my classes, where I frequently watched her calm and encourage other students with her easy laugh and sense of perspective. Joan graduated from UTSA with her BA in psychology.

NONTRADITIONAL STUDENT

We have just moved to Robins Air Force Base in Warner Robins, Georgia. Where is that, you ask? Sixty miles south of Atlanta, or "Bubbaville," as we lovingly call it. I feel like I've come full circle. Friends who know I moved from Lackland Air Force base in San Antonio, Texas ask how I like being here. I say I already know this side of the world. You see, I'm an Army brat whose father was stationed all over the United States, but mostly in the south. I was born in Fort Polk, Louisiana. My family lived at Fort Jackson, South Carolina twice, and in Gainesville, Georgia while I was in middle school and high school. Later, for almost eight years during and after my first marriage, I lived in Chattanooga, Tennessee.

Yep, I was used to living in southern states where most people thought I was "I-talian" (pronounced with a southern accent) or Greek because of my dark European features. That really translates to a large nose, olive skin, and brown eyes, but, unfortunately, not to looking like a Kardashian—more like the movie *My Big Fat Greek Wedding*. When we first moved to Gainesville, Georgia, I had long hair that I wore in pigtails and braids. My younger brother had a bowl cut, so he looked Asian to the locals. My parents are fair-skinned, so our last name of Cardenas did not raise any eyebrows regarding our Hispanic background. Most just pronounced it "Car- dean-ass" or "Gar-dean-as." Combine my look with a southern accent, and people didn't know *what* to think about my family's heritage. My family is from Texas, so moving to San Antonio and attending UTSA was, in a way, coming back home. However, I wasn't used to being part of the crowd and blending in with so many other Mexican Americans.

Both of my parents were born and raised in Austin, so that's where we lived while Dad served both of his Vietnam tours. I was closest to my Mexican heritage during those times, because Mom would take my brothers and me to my aunt's house to play with our cousins. She had eight children, so she made a bag of flour tortillas daily, and she could feed her family with what seemed like only a roasted jalapeño, a pot of pinto beans, and a little pork. Spanglish was spoken in my aunt's house, and Mexican music always played in the background. By contrast, my mother was convinced that speaking only English in our house—and fitting in to whichever community we lived in at the time—was very important to our education. After Dad returned from the war, we visited Texas only on vacation. I never learned Spanish fluently; I quickly found out that this is typical of my generation here in Texas.

I first started attending college at the University of Texas in Austin in 1982, but I didn't finish my degree then. Instead, I met an Army officer, got married, got pregnant, raised two children, and moved to five more states over the next fifteen years before divorcing and moving to San Antonio. I tried several times to go back to college over the years, but it was difficult during those years, with kids, a full-time job, and little support at home.

Almost thirty years later, I was fortunate enough to have my new husband, who is in the Air Force, transfer his 9/11 educational benefits to me. I was blessed in that I could finally afford to attend school full-time and finish my degree without having to work. An added bonus for me was that I would be a first-generation college graduate in my family. On my goal board at home, I had listed earning my diploma, with the intent to finish by the time I turned fifty and before my children completed their degrees. Although I did accomplish all of those things, I think the bigger value for me, in hindsight, was learning about myself and what I was capable of accomplishing mentally and academically.

My initial experiences at UTSA were positive but overwhelming: learning how to get on the Blackboard website (used to communicate with professors, turn in assignments, and connect with other students); figuring out how and where to use my UTSA identification card; and remembering passwords, logins, and different emails, etc., all while clearing cobwebs out of my brain to start retaining some of the information the professors spewed out those first few weeks, was interesting to say the least. I'd managed surgical centers and other offices with a staff of twenty, but I did not know if I could study properly or do well in school carrying a fifteen-credit-hour schedule. I was scared, and felt the same insecurities about attending school that I felt in high school or when I tried to return to college over the years.

I quickly learned that the mental "colored glasses" I was wearing determined my experiences and my outlook about my education at UTSA. For instance, both of my children are gifted and did not have to work at making good grades. My older brother was also gifted, and he skipped a grade. By contrast, I grew up believing I wasn't "smart" or good in math. I always thought I did my best, and still only made Bs. I felt intimidated by the younger college students and reverted to my old mentality about my ability level.

Two things changed my outlook about how I was going to perform in school. One day my husband asked me why I was settling for Bs when I didn't "settle" for anything while running a business. I expected excellence from my staff and myself. I realized then that if I wanted an A I was going to have to put in the effort. The second insight that solidified my resolve to expect an A for my efforts came after the third or fourth time one of the kids in class asked me for a pencil, asked which Scantron form (used for multiple choice tests) we needed on the day of a test, or asked a stupid question the night before an exam via Blackboard. Yes, asking which chapters are going to be covered on the test, the night before the test, is a stupid question! I realized then that if those kids could get by without studying and make a B or a C, I could certainly expect more of myself and get As!

When I was writing this, the movie, *The Butler* had just come out, and Martin Luther King was being celebrated for all of his accomplishments. African American history is certainly important, but, while watching the movie, I couldn't help but think about the hardships my parents and grandparents endured as first- and second-generation Mexicans in Texas. My mother picked cotton as a five-year-old, lost her mother to tuberculosis, and was not allowed on school buses or in the same restrooms with whites. Her uncles made fun of her for wanting to go to school, and didn't think a girl needed to attend school. The expectations her parents' generation had of women and men within the Mexican American community during the 1950s and '60s has made a lasting impression on schools and businesses to this day. In my personal experience, within my family and in the Austin and San Antonio community, I saw firsthand that low-income Hispanic family members and others who were raised with low expectations of themselves and their life possibilities often did not consider college to be an option.

When I was working full-time in a plastic surgery office, I often interviewed Mexican American women who did not easily look in my eyes. Some even admitted to being intimidated by working on the north side of San Antonio near a country club for "uppity" rich people. Several women reminded me of my mother and other relatives in their mannerisms and thought processes, and I knew they were a product of their upbringing. I have always considered myself lucky, though, because as an Army brat, I was able to see myself through others' eyes and to know I was not limited to expectations based on the color of my skin or my last name.

To me, UTSA was a melting pot of different ages, skin colors, levels of intelligence, and backgrounds. It felt like home, just like a military base does, in that comfort came from knowing we were all in the same boat. We all were there for an education and to grow as individuals. Maybe it was just time for me to learn and understand that my rose-colored glasses really are rosy, because I came full circle and was ready to accept and feel worthy of a college education.

San Antonio and UTSA are unique in that Mexican Americans are considered an important class of citizens that need the communities' help and attention as much as, as if not more than, other minority groups. The university furthermore shows support to nontraditional students, women, and veterans. I appreciated the way the Veterans Office at UTSA usually went above and beyond to help the veterans and their families. Most professors and staff were equally as professional and caring with us nontraditional students who were returning to school as they were toward the younger students attending college for the first time. My youngest son will attend UTSA, and I feel proud to be a graduate of UTSA. Go Road Runners!

MICHAEL HUEBNER
ARMY

Michael is a former combat medic, the father of a seven-year-old son, and was a former president of the Student Veterans Association (SVA) at the University of Texas at San Antonio (UTSA). As a student and veteran leader, he became the voice of veterans on campus. Whether presenting at panel discussions and committee meetings or simply talking with other students, his infectious enthusiasm and passion for helping veterans shined through. In one of my most memorable teaching moments, I asked him, during a Psychology and Health class, to talk about his experience as a medic. In a quiet voice, he held a class of over one hundred students spellbound as he talked about the pain and courage he had seen. When discussing that moment later, Michael and I both realized that in telling their stories, both verbally and through their actions, veterans have a great deal to share with us.

A STORY OF PERSISTENCE:
"SUPERMAN OR NOT, WAR CHANGES YOU"

I grew up in a middle class family that lived all over Texas: in Austin, Houston, San Antonio, Colleyville, Harlingen, Donna, and Fort Worth. I always did well in school and graduated in the top 10 percent of my high school class, but I didn't receive any college scholarships. My parents were divorced, so I didn't have enough resources to go to college. I needed a future, and because I had two stepbrothers in the military, I chose to enlist in the United States Army.

After basic training in Fort Leonard Wood, Missouri, in 1997, I followed up with training for my Military Occupation (MOS), and was assigned to take a Medical Specialist Course for my Advanced Individual Training (AIT) in Fort Sam Houston, Texas. After completion, my first duty station was as a line medic in Giessen, Germany.

As a line medic, I was put in charge of responding to the entire company's medical diagnosis and treatment. This included handling the medications for routine conditions such as colds, the flu, diarrhea, nausea and vomiting, pain management, dehydration sickness, and cold weather injuries. On several occasions I had to use my emergency medical skills and training to help soldiers who had real-world, life-threatening injuries. After gaining experience and education as a combat medic, I became field sanitation certified and was put in charge of the curriculum and training for all the Combat Lifesavers in the Battalion.

Subsequently, I went to the Evans Army Community Hospital (USA MEDDAC, a Level II Trauma Hospital) in Fort Carson, Colorado, where I worked in the Emergency Medical Department as a supervisor. This gave me the opportunity to enhance my skills as a Health Care Specialist. As my skills increased, so did my responsibilities: I became suture certified (suturing children, deep tissue, faces, etc.), and performed difficult IV and phlebotomy tasks around the hospital for both pediatric and geriatric patients. I also gained the technical skills to perform Registered Nurse tasks within the emergency department and ambulance services.

While I was developing my medical skills, I also tried several times to start attending college. I enrolled in the University of Maryland while stationed in Germany, but had to withdraw because of field training exercises. Later, I took several courses at Pikes Peak Community College at Fort Carson and at Honolulu Community College at Schofield Barracks. In addition, I trained in trauma care at Fort Carson and became one of the first Advanced Combat Medics in the Army.

I reenlisted in the Army for another four years and received radiology training at Fort Sam Houston. After completing that training, I was stationed as a Radiology Technologist in a forward support battalion at Schofield Barracks, Hawaii. I also worked in the radiology departments at the medical treatment facility at Schofield Barracks and at Tripler Army Medical

Center in Hawaii to enhance my knowledge of radiology techniques and advanced radiography procedures.

While stationed in Hawaii, I attended a Primary Leadership Development Course (PLDC) in preparation for my promotion to Sergeant, which would include more leadership responsibilities. PLDC taught me the Army way of life as a leader and honed my skills to lead from the front and take charge. The course increased my knowledge and understanding of military order, discipline, history, tactics, and training methods.

All of my medical and military training came into play when I was deployed to Kandahar, Afghanistan from 2004–2005. I was promoted to Sergeant/E-5 and served as a supervisor in both the radiology department and the orthopedic clinic. We provided treatment for both coalition forces and local national patients. We were responsible for radiographing all detainees for tuberculosis as well as all radiographic imaging for the hospital. Because of my training in multiple medical modalities, I worked on the trauma team and continued treating patients from the flight line to post-operative care and throughout the recovery process.

As a medic, I also conducted (CMAX) humanitarian aid missions in the local Afghanistan villages around Kandahar. The conditions in Afghanistan were grim, and the entire tour was a whirl of blood and death. I lost numerous personal friends and fellow soldiers. I still recall the days of being shot at and witnessing nightmarish scenes in operating rooms that led to sleepless nights. When people ask me about my experiences, all I can say is that it was horrific. It changes a man.

After separating from the military at the end of 2005, I attempted to complete my college degree at the University of Texas at Arlington. However, at that time undiagnosed Post-Traumatic Stress Disorder (PTSD) controlled my life. My first attempt to obtain employment at a hospital made me vomit because of the antiseptic smell which brought back my memories and nightmares from Afghanistan. This made it impossible to find a job using my medical skills. In addition, I had no support there, and I couldn't seem to connect with other students. Finally, the Department of Veterans Affairs (VA) diagnosed me with depression and PTSD. It took over five years of psychological treatment, but I eventually reentered school at the University of Texas at San Antonio (UTSA) in 2010.

There I slowly made friends with other veterans, found my footing academically, and decided to major in psychology and sociology. I also joined a group of veterans and psychology students who were conducting research on the needs of veteran students at UTSA. This group, the Veteran Scholars Program, developed a series of workshops to be offered to incoming veterans on topics such as finding an academic mentor, managing time effectively, and coping with stress. We also did a number of presentations on campus, and even did a panel discussion on student veterans' issues at the Southwestern Psychological Association (SWPA) meeting held in San Antonio.

I was also elected to be the president of the Student Veterans Association at UTSA. The UTSA chapter of the national organization focuses on helping veterans find resources, guidance, and access to veterans affairs counselors at the university. As president, I also worked to influence university policies regarding vets and to establish a veteran's center. Additionally, we reached out to satellite campuses and local universities to form a support network for area veterans.

Unfortunately, my time at UTSA was not always easy. It was a constant struggle to earn enough money to cover my financial needs and still provide for my son. At one point, my housing situation fell apart, and I lived in my car for over a week. This time, though, I had friends on campus who helped me find a place to live, and refused to let me isolate myself and give up. In the spring of 2014, I graduated with my bachelor's degree in psychology.

In the end, my eight-plus years of military service have both helped and hindered me in my endeavors to achieve a higher education. It took me fifteen years to complete my degree. However, I plan to continue my education by pursuing a master's degree and a PhD in Psychology. My future goal is to work for the VA developing treatments and, hopefully, cures for soldiers with mental health disorders resulting from military service.

JENNIFER HALL
MARINES

When teaching large classes, it can take several weeks to figure out which students are willing to speak up and express their feelings. However, it only took me a class or two to realize that Jenna could be counted on to share her military experiences and express her feelings with honesty and confidence. Therefore, I was not surprised to hear that after graduating she used her criminal justice and psychology degrees to obtain a job with Child Protective Services here in Texas. She is now using her formidable leadership skills to advocate for the most vulnerable members of our communities.

People ask me why in the world I joined the Marines. Of all the branches, why did I choose the Marines? My reply has always been, "Why not?" I wanted to prove to myself I could do it, and I did. Don't get me wrong: there were times when I was cursing myself out for the choice I had made, but looking back, I don't regret it. Yes, there were times I did not like it, but I am glad I had the courage to push myself onto an incredible journey.

I was in junior college when I began feeling restless. I had been in school for two years already, and I didn't know what I wanted to do. I had grand dreams of traveling the world, having a college education (something no one else in my family had, other than one aunt), and living an incredible life with a job I wanted to wake up to every single day—loving my life in general. But I didn't know how to do that. I was living with my grandparents and an aunt at the time, and though I was happy, I was lonely and, as I said before, I began to feel restless. I was studying for nursing school, but I was not getting the grades I needed to get there. I was floundering, not knowing what I was going to do with my life.

One night I was talking to a friend of mine, and she mentioned that she had gone into the Marines. I thought, "Why not? That could be me." After all, after September 11th, I had almost joined the military, so it wasn't a new concept for me to consider.

So I went to speak to a recruiter myself. There were three recruiters in the office, which is pretty typical. The unusual thing, though, was that this little town happened to have a female recruiter, and that made a world of difference. The male recruiters instantly dismissed me. They actually told me that the Navy recruiters next door would be happy to sign me up, but that I wasn't what the Marines were looking for. Well, I don't know about you, but when someone tells me I can't do something, I am going to do what it takes to prove to them that I can!

Just because I happened to be a tall woman with some extra weight, the male recruiters dismissed me as a lost cause. But not Sergeant April Skinner (now Scarbourgh). She told me exactly what it would take to be a female in the Marines, especially the first couple of years. Then she took me back to the scale, we figured out how much weight I would have to lose before I could even be screened for possible enlistment, and we came up with a plan to help me lose the weight. Before that day, I had not run if it was not required to save my life. After that day—well, let's just say that my knees aren't happy with me most of the time.

Six weeks later, with the help of Sgt. Skinner, I was in Dallas enlisting in the Marines. It was November 10, 2003, the Marine Corps birthday, though I did not know it at that time. It would be another few weeks before my family even knew I had talked to a recruiter, let alone enlisted.

I left for boot camp on February 23, 2004. All I remember from the first few days was sitting around drinking water while the platoon as a whole went through detox (nicotine, alcohol, caffeine), was issued gear, and learned what was expected. Before I joined the training platoon, however, I was dropped into a medical unit because I had several large, unexplained, black bruises on my legs. I spent the next six weeks undergoing medical testing to ensure that I didn't have cancer or some sort of condition that would require me to leave the Marines. It wasn't until after boot camp, when I had my medical records in my hands, that I finally learned that I have a bleeding disorder. Although it wasn't severe enough to require medication or discharge from service, I do need to be careful of surgeries and any major cuts.

Boot camp was definitely a culture shock—everything you ever hear about—yet I also had some of the most exhilarating moments in my life there. For example, in the last battalion, I was put in the front of the platoon and managed to stay there for the entire run (did I mention that I am *not* a runner yet?). I still remember the "Ooh-Rah" I received from my senior drill instructor when I was able to do the rope obstacle without winding up in the water below, as well as the look of utter disbelief on my kill-hat's face when I was able to do the zigzagged height-changing monkey bars in a matter of seconds. Just in case you are curious, a kill-hat (or heavy) is the one drill instructor who is the hardest on you, wears you down the most, and always seems to be riding you. I even earned the highest-level swim qualification offered in the Marine Corps without going for swim-qualified instructor.

The female sergeant scared the devil out of me ninety-nine percent of the time I was in boot camp, but she was always the one pushing me, never letting me give up on myself—something I will always be grateful for. I spent my birthday there, which my sister accidently ensured everyone knew when my birthday card arrived in the mail, decorated all over the outside with "Happy 21st," beer bottles, and champagne glasses. Definitely not a day I will ever forget, and not for the normal reasons. At the end of boot camp, when my mother, brother, aunt, and several friends drove to South Carolina to see me graduate, none of them recognized me. I had lost a lot of weight in less than five months, and I carried myself in a whole new manner.

After boot camp, I went home for ten days before heading to Marine Combat Training (MCT). Those ten days were full of great memories, and I will never forget the reactions of friends and family who walked right past me without seeing me. It was an amazing feeling. It wasn't just the weight loss; it was my entire carriage and presence.

Upon arrival at Camp Geiger, North Carolina, I began MCT. This was a twenty-three-day training, with seventeen of those spent in the field, learning the different weapons and firing them. Though the heat and humidity were miserable (July in North Carolina is *not* fun), I was having a blast throwing grenades, shooting caliber machine guns, and even getting to shoot a bazooka. Unfortunately, I ended the training with a broken foot, so back into a medical platoon I went for six weeks until it healed. I had finished that nine-mile hike in from the field with not only a broken foot, but also a broken shoulder strap on my pack (thank God for duct tape).

Upon checking into my first unit at Camp Lejeune, North Carolina, in November, I was told not to get too comfortable because I would be deploying in three short months. So, in late February/early March, I left the world as I knew it and headed to a destination on the other side of the world. I spent almost seven months there, made some amazing friends (as well as some of my worst memories), and turned twenty-two half a world away from everyone I loved.

It was the end of September when I returned to the States, and the Green Day song, "Wake Me Up When September Ends" was more than highly appropriate for my life at that point. I spent my next birthday somewhere on the road between North Carolina and Texas for a few days of leave prior to heading to my new base in Kaneohe Bay, Hawaii. I won't make you jealous and expand upon how I spent the next months in absolute heaven, or how, when I wasn't working or training with the Marines, I was all over that island exploring, snorkeling, sunbathing, swimming, and riding my motorcycle or driving my topless, doorless Jeep in paradise. But life continued on, and four years after I had left for boot camp, I returned to civilian life. Again, I floundered. The skills I obtained in the Marine Corps were not easily transferred into civilian life. I had training in embarkation and logistics, and only major companies like FedEx, UPS, or the Postal Service had a need for those kinds of skills. But that wasn't what I wanted to do in my life anyway.

I went to work as a bartender and at a Babies 'R Us store. I also began applying for colleges in Texas with criminal justice degree programs, and eighteen months after I left the Marines, I entered the University of Texas at San Antonio (UTSA) as a criminal justice major. Because I had two and a half years of junior college, along with credits from the Marine Corps, I transferred into the school (unfortunately, with a low GPA), just nine credits shy of being a junior. I didn't have to attend orientation, and I didn't choose to. I knew what to expect, and I did not want to spend four days in a dorm with eighteen-year-old girls who didn't know what they were doing there and who were more worried about the cute boys. While I don't regret it, I wish I had been offered a transfer type of orientation just to discover the hidden secrets of the campus.

Because I'm a veteran, I was able to use my GI Bill to pay for school, and I was given a monthly stipend to assist with living expenses. The initial problem was that, every single semester, the Department of Veterans Affairs (VA) is overrun with students requesting assistance, and if you haven't certified before, you don't know that it takes weeks for it to kick in and you start to receive payments. There wasn't a veterans' class to help those of us coming to the school learn these things. My father loaned me some money in the beginning so I could move my stuff to San Antonio, put a deposit on an apartment, and pay for other living expenses until my stipend kicked in, finally, at the end of October.

Since I was accepted into UTSA so late (August 11), I only had a week and a half to register, meet with an advisor, get a schedule, and apply for the GI Bill. And on top of that, I still had to move! I had never felt more alone. I was in a new city where I didn't know anyone, on a campus with tens of thousands of students (much different from my small little junior college that covered only one square block). Slowly, though, I began making friends.

You know that first day of class, when the professors have you stand up, say your name, where you are from, what your major is, and anything else about yourself? As much as I hated that, I was grateful for it, because it helped me identify other veterans in my classes. I always tried to take note of any veteran, especially other Marines. I began to engage them in conversations so that I would have someone to talk to who had the same mind-set as mine—people I could trust to work with on a group project because I knew they would actually complete the task without slacking off.

It wasn't anything against the other students, but I just found that the majority of the older students tended to be veterans, and I had a hard time relating to the eighteen-year-old, fresh-from-high-school students. College for them was an adventure; college for me was something I had fought for. I wasn't there because Mommy and Daddy could afford to send me there; I had had to sacrifice four years of my life to be able to afford to do it (a sacrifice I was glad to make).

I met many of my veteran friends from school because we shared classes. And once I had a class with someone, especially if it was a major-related class, I always tried to get other classes with them. In fact, for eighteen months straight, another Marine, Jason, and I always had at least one class together. At one point we had three in one semester, and we ended up graduating together. I honestly think the only reason I made the grade in one of my classes was because of him.

It was during my first semester that I realized I wanted to expand upon my degree, and I added psychology as a second major. After having a bad professor my first semester, I did the smart thing and began researching professors online before enrolling in their classes.

I had registered online for my second semester of school, but it didn't matter. Due to a backlog of claims in the VA system, the school never received confirmation that I was a veteran who would be covered by the VA. All my classes were dropped just days prior to the start of the new semester, and I could not register for four more days. From what I was hearing on campus, I was one of many who were affected by this. In fact, the college has since changed the way they process veterans because so many people had complained about losing the classes they needed to graduate

The entire time I was in college, it seemed like one uphill battle after another with the VA. One spring semester, I was struggling in a mandatory Research and Design for Psychology class which had a required lab. In order to be considered full time and receive the full stipend, you must take twelve credit hours, so I couldn't drop the class. In the end, I had to accept an F in the class so I could afford to live and continue on to graduation. Since it was a mandatory course, I had to drop all my summer classes, get written approval from all the professors to take their classes over the summer, and then obtain written approval from all the fall professors to take their classes in conjunction with retaking the Research and Design class (with a different professor, of course!). I was not able to take some of the classes I wanted to, simply because the professors wouldn't allow it. It was very stressful several months for me. Doctor McNaughton-Cassill was a lifesaver. She allowed me into her summer class, her fall class, and her fall research internship to give me the classes and credits I needed. She became a not-too-silent voice in my head, pushing me at the end of the race when I wasn't sure I was going to have the energy or ability to finish.

I spent a total of two and a half years at UTSA and received a double bachelor's degree in criminal justice and psychology simultaneously: I graduated on a Thursday *and* a Saturday in December 2011. All the stress endured, all the trauma suffered, and every ounce of grief was worth it to get those diplomas, and once again prove to myself I could do something that someone told me I could not do, and achieve a dream I thought was once unobtainable.

ANA GONZALEZ
ARMY

Ana's diminutive size and flawless manners camouflage her core strength and determination. Whether she was battling discrimination, raising her children while her husband was stationed in another state, earning top grades, and serving as the public relations officer for the UTSA Student Veterans Association, she never lost sight of her desire to become a voice for other women, and for veterans.

MY STORY AS A SOLDIER, MOTHER, WIFE, AND STUDENT!

All I remember was riding a bus to Fort Jackson, South Carolina. I was sitting next to a girl who had become my friend for the last few hours, and I was terrified—not only because I was afraid of what training would be like, but also because I was away from my children. However, I kept telling myself to be strong and keep focused on my children.

Once we arrived at Fort Jackson, a drill sergeant came onto the bus yelling at all of us to get off. I didn't understand why he had to yell so much and why all the sergeants had such bad attitudes. I thought it was unnecessary and somewhat pointless; after all, I was a grown, responsible woman with a family back home. As the night progressed, the sergeants kept yelling about what we could and couldn't do. They also kept us up most of the night, allowing us to sleep for only about an hour.

The following day was nothing but standing around. Everywhere we went and everything we did involved standing like robots in lines. The first few days were difficult for me because everything was different; I had to watch how I talked, when I talked, and where I went. I even had to watch what I ate at the dining facility, since desserts were completely off limits. The drill sergeants were just waiting for somebody to make a mistake; they loved ridiculing, putting down, and scaring soldiers in order to feed their own egos.

After about a week, we were put onto white buses and ordered to put our heads down with our eyes closed; they told us not to dare to look up. I think they drove us around for about twenty minutes, making us believe we were far away from the rest of civilization on base, which just added to our anxiety and uncertainty.

Things only got harder as time went on. I didn't have contact with my family, and I was living with a lot of females from different backgrounds, religions, and ethnicities. All of us were on edge, sharing the same experiences but being affected by them differently, and soon there was enough drama to drive anybody insane.

Basic Combat Training (BCT) was wearing me out emotionally; not only was I adjusting to the training and strict regime, but I was also dealing with my husband, who I thought was acting irresponsibly. He even left town on a Friday and forgot to pick up my son from school; fortunately, my mother was later called to pick my son up.

As hard as it was getting used to all the rules and new Army structure, dealing with my husband was even more difficult because I couldn't do anything from where I was. I just had to wait, hearing about his reckless actions in letters from my mom and my weekly calls home. Eventually, I started to question myself and my ability to stay in the military. Fortunately, I formed strong friendships with other female soldiers who helped me get through BCT. I realized that, out of all the things I had heard about the military, developing close, strong friendships was the one thing that everyone seemed to agree on.

I thought Advanced Individual Training would be easier than basic training, and in some respects it was. For the first week and a half, it was pretty relaxed. We were allowed to go to the store and some other places on post, and we also had plenty of free time to socialize with other soldiers. For the first time in a long time, I felt like things were getting better. However, when our EMT training started, I felt like I was right back in basic training, but I decided to try to make the best of it.

I fought to stay focused. I was having a hard time staying awake in EMT class and struggling to find enough motivation to be a good soldier. I started to see the Army as a wall between my children and me. Every day was a constant struggle: I would wake up with the intention to be a better soldier and to find a way to stand out from the rest of my peers. But, as the day progressed, my motivation would fade out, and my frustration and sense of hopelessness would take over. In the meantime, I was assigned to move to Fort Polk. The problem was that I didn't have anybody to care for my children because there was a long waiting list for child care. To cope, I reconciled with my husband, and we moved to Louisiana together.

When we first got to Fort Polk, it was a culture shock; the only nearby town had nothing but a Walmart. Unfortunately, the situation with my husband got so bad that one night I had no choice but to call the police. Shockingly, I was told one of us had to leave the house and we had to be apart for at least seventy-two hours to let things "cool down" and prevent a tragedy. Since I was the soldier, and not he, I had to leave the house. They called my supervisor, who came to pick me up.

I was furious that I had to leave, but I had no choice. I grabbed my uniforms and personal items and left the house. I was put in a barracks room for three days with no contact with him or my children. Soon, all kinds of rumors started to go around. I even heard people saying I had been beaten up by my husband.

Fortunately, though, I started to get more comfortable in my unit. They were very focused on physical training (PT), and were quite competitive, which was something I was able to take advantage of. I was soon known as the fastest female in my company. I tried to socialize with other soldiers in my unit, both on and off duty. I frequently had gatherings at my house, and we all became quite close.

As the holidays approached, I planned to go back to Colombia and visit my family. I requested a few weeks of leave, but apparently Columbia was on a blacklist of countries where soldiers aren't allowed to go. I was further told that as a Colombian citizen, I also ran the risk of being used to obtain information if someone knew I was a soldier. Although I had made the conscious choice to join and "give up my life to the Army," I never imagined that I'd had no say in something so personal and basic as being able to visit my family. I was in shock—I had spent close to $3000 on tickets alone! Thankfully, my leave was finally approved.

At that time, I was also tasked to the Soldiers Readiness Processing (SRP) center. My duties included administering immunizations and inputting data into personnel medical files. I truly enjoyed my job there; the work environment was fun yet professional. Unfortunately, the situation with my husband continued to deteriorate, and we separated again, making it difficult to balance my work and child care. When my children were sick and I had to miss work, my leaders grew suspicious. They began to think that I was lying to them or taking advantage of my daughter's custody plan.

Meanwhile, I was tasked to work at the hospital once again. This time, I was in family medicine, working mostly with civilian nurses. I did really well there, and I enjoyed working with soldiers' families. My work and dedication was well appreciated at the clinic. The nurses often thanked me for going out of my way to help out, and I met someone (another military member) who I felt loved and supported me for who I was.

It felt like everything was falling into place until one morning as I was dropping off my son at "before school" care on-post: I wasn't allowed to leave him there because his allergy plan wasn't updated, even though they had my son's EpiPen prescription on site. I immediately informed my NCO, telling him that I'd be in formation with my son.

I showed up to formation on time as usual, and told the NCO that I had to wait for the Child, Youth, and School Services (CYS) office to open so that I could update my son's allergy plan. I was excused after formation to handle the situation. I was there shortly after the CYS office opened, but I had to wait for a while before seeing anyone. While I was waiting, another soldier from my section showed up looking for me. He approached me and told me he just wanted to make sure I was fine. Really? Why wouldn't I be? He shook his head and told me he was sorry, but that he had basically been sent to "babysit" me and make sure that I wasn't making up a story about my son's medication issues.

In the meantime, my estimated time of separation from the military got closer. I was glad I was able to see the light at the end of the tunnel. I knew that if I stayed in Fort Polk I wasn't going to be able to finish my degree. There were only a couple of schools that offered lower-division classes, and I only needed upper-division courses. Everybody in my family is a college grad, and in some way I felt ashamed I wasn't done yet. In the end, I decided that I would return to San Antonio to finish school and wait for my new partner to complete his military commitment.

I was accepted to UTSA, and we bought a new house. Once I was in San Antonio, everything was so different. I was living in a hotel room with dogs and kids while the house was being built. I had only a few days to register the kids in school and get us settled in before I started school at UTSA. When I was finally able to close on the house, it felt like a dream come true. My partner and I were so happy that we decided to get married by a Justice of the Peace, with the intention of having a bigger wedding later on.

I had heard that UTSA was a big school, so I went on campus the day before classes started just to find out where I could park and where my classrooms were going to be. It took me a while to figure everything out on my own. I knew I should've gone through orientation, but as a transfer student I didn't have to. The classroom numbers almost looked like land navigation coordinates (e.g., 2.09.23). I thought that place was ridiculous; it was too big, and there were too many students.

The first few weeks in school were awkward. I couldn't relate to anybody, I was older than most students, and I had a family. There were so many people around me, yet I felt so lonely. I only went to class, then back to the hotel; I didn't want to interact with people, and I often felt confused and lost.

I also had to report to my reserve unit. During my first drill, I found out I was put in a slot for a dialysis tech, not for just a medic. My new commander seemed really nice. However, the amount of personal pressure I felt to complete my degree was greater. At school, I was still not interacting with anybody. I also noticed that during the first few weeks of school, everybody showed up to class, but towards the middle of the semester, about half the class was still attending. I thought, "What a waste of time and money; why bother with college if they weren't going to come to class?" It also felt weird to realize that if I didn't want to come to class, no one would say anything. I didn't have to report to anybody, I didn't have to explain anything, and I didn't have to show any appointment slips or doctor's notes. In that sense, it felt good to have that much freedom, but on the other hand, it was kind of scary to think how easy it might be to fall in that category of students who only come to class on test day.

I managed to survive the first semester; I attended all my classes (with a couple of exceptions when I had an appointment) and did well on my finals, but I realized I was pursuing something I wasn't passionate about. Fortunately, I was on time to make that change, and by the beginning of the next semester, I had decided to switch majors. I had analyzed what I really wanted to do, where I wanted to be, and what it would take me to get there.

I decided to pursue law school, so when I started getting e-mail invitations to join different student organizations, I decided to give it a try, even though I thought I'd feel out of place. I joined a couple of organizations, met other students, and got involved in student activities. It was hard to balance the requirements for those organizations along with five courses, being in the reserve, and being a mom; however, somehow, I managed to do it all. In addition, I was lucky enough to join a research group looking at the student veteran experience at UTSA. From then on, I was more involved in school.

Towards the end of the semester, I decided to volunteer for a leadership position with the Student Veterans Association, and I was elected to be the Public Affairs Officer. I didn't take on this role only because it would make my law school application look better, but because I really wanted to make a difference in the organization and possibly help other veterans take advantage of everything the school has to offer. Things were looking up for me; I never thought I would be so involved in school and be presented with so many opportunities. I was also accepted in the Summer Law School Preparation Academy, an intense but fulfilling summer program designed to help students get familiarized with law school coursework. I received a certificate in legal reasoning at the completion of the program.

Adding to my list of school responsibilities, I decided to take on the role of Vice President for Alpha Chi National Honors Society, an organization that recognizes the top 10 percent of junior, senior, and graduate students. It was a complete honor, yet another challenge, since I didn't want to let anybody down.

During the fall semester, I was committed to all my school activities and to the law school application process. It wasn't an easy semester; my kids required more attention with their homework and school activities, in addition to all my schoolwork and student activities. As Vice President and Public Affairs Officer for my organizations, I planned all social, service, and volunteering events, and I managed most of the correspondence. It honestly was more that I bargained for, but I liked what I did.

Right before finals, my reserve unit told me I needed to do my annual medic training, which I hadn't done in almost two years. Unfortunately, it was a week-long training held on exactly the same days as finals. My mother, who usually helps me at home with the kids, was going to Colombia during that time. I was waking up around 3:30 a.m. to drive my kids to my sister-in-law's home so she could watch them. By the time I got home to make dinner and help my kids with their homework, I was always too tired to study. It was literally one of the worst weeks of my life. I wasn't able to focus on the training because I was too worried about finals, and I couldn't concentrate when I studied at night because I was so tired.

In the end, everything worked out. I'm just glad I was able to accomplish it all. I had the opportunity to present our Veteran Scholar Program (VSP) at a symposium at the Southwestern Psychological Association annual conference; I am also going to present the module I've been working on for the VSP at the Alpha Chi annual conference in St. Louis, Missouri.

Lastly, I'm getting ready to accomplish my biggest goal of all by graduating this semester. Although I started school at UTSA with a completely different outlook, I couldn't be happier with the way things turned out. Everything happens for a reason, and I can only learn from all those experiences in the military which made me stronger and gave me the determination I needed to succeed in all aspects of my life. I have the best husband I could possibly ask for; his support and love has helped me reach my goals. I have no regrets, and I would do it all over again.

NATHAN HODGE
ARMY

Nathan is a big guy who can't help but look uncomfortable when wedged into a small plastic chair with an attached desk. Nevertheless, he is quick to smile, enthusiastic about learning, and always generous in his support of others. Since graduating from UTSA, he has taken a job at USAA, the military insurance company.

I often think of my journey through college and the Army as being a long and unique one. I was born at Walter Reed Army Medical Center in Washington, DC, and both of my parents were United States Army officers. My father retired as a lieutenant colonel in December of 1995, and my mother left the Army as a captain when she became pregnant with me. My father finished two master's degrees, and my mother finished her bachelor's degree. When I was thirteen, my mother died of cancer; as a result, I struggled through high school. I graduated in 1996 and moved with my father up to the Nashville area.

My first semester in college was in the spring of 1997 at Columbia State Community College (just south of Nashville), and it was a disaster. I was not ready to dedicate myself to the workload that I was going to have to endure as a college student, and I was still feeling burned out from my struggles in high school. In the summer of 1997, I decided to enlist in the Army. I started basic training in November of that year, and I spent from March of 1998 until November of 2000 stationed at Ft. Bragg, North Carolina.

During my final year at Ft. Bragg, I developed a plan: I was going to go into the Army Reserves, work my way through school at San Antonio College, transfer to the University of Texas at San Antonio, join the ROTC program, and become an Army officer. I was not sure about what my major would be, but I thought I could figure that out later.

My first semester at San Antonio College in the spring of 2001 was pretty successful, and I made fairly good grades. However, I started to notice a lot of differences between my time on active duty compared with my time as a college student and Army reservist. For the most part, during my active duty time, we worked together as a team. We were always training, and we had the comradery that comes with being on active duty.

As a reservist and college student here in San Antonio, though, things were quite different. I eventually realized that there was no comradery in the reserves; we were supposed to be a Tier One unit—highly deployable—yet we never trained. In college, I realized that, for the most part, I was on my own. Everybody in college was there to help him or herself.

At the end of the 2001 spring semester, I took a job at a Hollywood Video store and, even though I was still getting the GI Bill and was getting paid as a reservist, I started to struggle financially. Eventually, I found myself working more hours at the store just to pay my increasing bills. As a result, my grades began to drop substantially, and I eventually found myself following a frustrating pattern: I would sign up for classes, only to drop them halfway through the semester. In the summer of 2002, I became tired of how my reserve unit was being run, so I left and went onto inactive reserve. In 2003, I took an unarmed security job, but I was still stuck in the pattern of dropping classes in school.

In the summer of 2004, the Army called me back to active duty, and I was deployed to Kuwait as part of Operation Iraqi Freedom. I spent two weeks in Kuwait before I was sent back to the United States with a bad back. I was eventually sent to Walter Reed Army Medical Center, where I spent almost eight months receiving chiropractic treatment and physical therapy.

While I was recovering, I spent a lot of free time thinking about what I wanted to do with the rest of my life. I had thought a lot about becoming a law enforcement officer, and I also seriously considered a career in psychology, but I was still not sure how I was going to get through school.

When I received my Honorable Discharge in October 2005, I left the Army determined to finish what I had started in college, so I moved back to San Antonio and went back to work at my previous security job. It was not until 2008, however, that I went back to take classes at San Antonio College, and it wasn't until the next year that I actually started to succeed.

I took three classes—College Algebra (for the fifth time), Introduction to Psychology, and a United States Government class. I finished with a B in Algebra and an A in Introduction to Psychology, but I dropped the government class. However, because of the good grades I did make, I was able to develop the confidence that if I dedicated myself to college, I could accomplish what I wanted.

I decided that semester to make psychology my official major. I started making better grades as time went by, and by the time I reached my final semester at San Antonio College, I was involved with the Psychology Club and making all As and Bs. I have not dropped a class since the fall of 2009, and I finished my associate's degree in psychology in the spring of 2012.

My first semester at the University of Texas at San Antonio was during the summer of 2012. I have occasionally struggled with my grades, but I have made the honor roll twice, and my grade point average has continued to improve. I have been involved with the Psychology Club, and I am scheduled to graduate this December (2014).

What I want to emphasize to other veterans who are entering college for the first time is that they have to have a vision and be willing to stick with it. There will be times when you will question whether or not you can succeed, and it is important to know that being in college means that, as a veteran, you may spend more time alone than you are used to. You may not know who to turn to when you need help, but it is important to figure that out. Other college students are in school to improve their own personal situations and might not be willing to be helpful to others.

Being a college student also requires patience and endurance. There will be times when, as a student, you get worn out and you do not want to study any more. It is important to keep pushing through those hard times and continue to study. It is also important to know when to take a break.

UNIT 3

3

LIFE AFTER GRADUATION

SANDRA PAHL
NAVAL PSYCHOLOGIST

I feel privileged to have had the opportunity to watch Sandra mature from an anxious undergraduate student to a confident Clinical Psychologist who earned her MA and her PhD in clinical psychology at UT Austin. Sandra, a former military spouse, is now herself a proud Navy Psychologist who is using her skills, perseverance, and personal strength to help other soldiers cope and reach their own potential. She currently serves as a Navy Psychologist in Quantico, VA.

ORANGE BLUE, ORANGE WHITE, BLUE AND GOLD: TRANSITIONING FROM STUDENT TO SAILOR

GROWING UP — DREAMS CHANGE

From the first time I watched an airplane launch off an aircraft carrier, I wanted to be a pilot. But as fate would have it, at age fifteen I was informed that my eyesight was very poor and I would never qualify for pilot training. After giving it some thought, I decided that clinical psychology would be an acceptable alternative choice; it would not only give me flexibility in terms of my professional path, it would also offer me the opportunity to join the military if I chose to do so. Many people had their doubts about my ability to complete a PhD, but persistence and hard work pay off.

My experiences are likely somewhat different from most veterans. Unlike many of our returning veterans, I joined the US Navy at age thirty-three with an almost-completed doctoral degree in clinical psychology from the University of Texas at Austin. Unlike many other service members, I have fulfilled roles as both the spouse of a service member and as an active duty service member myself. I've been a military wife, a student, a teacher, and a sailor, and I hope that because of these experiences, my story will resonate with many readers.

I grew up in a military family. My father served for twenty years before taking a position in the civilian world. For him, the transition from active duty to civilian life was a big adjustment. The military had been his life; having served on the enlisted as well as on the officer side, he knew both worlds, and he had enjoyed this lifestyle for two decades. To this day, my father is proud of his service and speaks fondly of his time on active duty.

Although I frequently hear about military children being brought up in a strict environment, this certainly was not true in my case. However, as is typical in most military families, my father was frequently away from home for training, so it was left to my mother to raise three children with very different personalities: my older brother, who was not only an exemplary student but also highly organized, and who would likely have done very well in the military; my younger brother, who is kind and caring but had difficulties with rules and regulation growing up, so he was an unlikely match for military service; and me, the middle child and only girl, who was characterized as obstinate and opinionated—a character trait that would later earn me the nickname "Objection."

Even as a young child, I usually spoke my mind when I believed it was necessary; this trait was fostered by my mother, a very independent and intelligent woman who, although always cognizant and supportive of my father's career, would speak her mind when necessary. My own outspokenness at times got me in trouble, especially with my father; although he is a very kind man, he occasionally had difficulty separating his professional life from his personal life, and occasionally he would resort to treating us children in a way that was reminiscent of how he dealt with recruits. During those times, it was my mother who gently reminded him that we were a family and that he needed to change his approach with his children.

In my father's defense, occasionally I would bring even my mother to the brink of insanity. I recall one particular occasion when I refused to greet the commanding officer's wife because "I did not like her." Even my patient mother became a little exasperated by my behavior and attempted to explain to me that even if I don't like a person, I could still be courteous. Of course, she was right.

Although at times common courtesies, neatness, and structure appeared to be lost on me, my parents raised me with the values that would later become the cornerstone of my Navy life: honor, courage, and commitment. To me, this means doing the right thing, even when it's the hard thing to do; respecting regulations and orders, but not blindly; and questioning decisions when necessary.

ORANGE BLUE – UNIVERSITY OF TEXAS AT SAN ANTONIO

Much to my parents' dismay, at the age of eighteen I married my first husband, who was an E-4 in the US Army. Since I was so young and still had not completed my education, my parents were less than happy about this development; however, true to their philosophy, they allowed me to make my own decisions. My husband received new orders to Fort Sam Houston shortly after we got married, and after graduation, we relocated to San Antonio, several thousand miles away from home. Many people who are not in the military fail to realize the challenges associated with a military lifestyle: there are no regular work hours; there is no overtime pay; there are frequent moves, and there is always the possibility of a deployment.

With his busy work schedule and his own problems to take care of, my husband was unable to help me choose, let alone enroll in, a college. San Antonio is the home of several universities, private and public. In the end, I chose to attend the University of Texas at San Antonio (UTSA), in part because it was a public school; I had graduated from a private high school and wanted a change of pace.

Moreover, UTSA was a large school. I loved the campus, with its setting just outside the city. I enrolled in the fall of 1999, and by the spring of 2000, I was a full-time student. I quickly realized that college would be labor intensive but not as much of a challenge as I had anticipated. I vowed to learn everything I could and to focus on my studies. I loved school, and I made friends more quickly than I had expected. In the summer of 2000, I met Dr. McNaughton-Cassill, who eventually became my mentor as well as the pillar of my sanity.

As much as I loved school, I could not ignore the problems outside the quiet halls of UTSA. San Antonio is a military town, and, like many students at the time, I was not the only one with life challenges. As I already mentioned, life as a military family, especially an enlisted one, is challenging. Living on the sole income of an E-4 was not easy. There was a necessity for two cars, along with an apartment, household expenses, tuition, books—you name it—but somehow we made it work. Although nonmilitary families were facing similar stressors, we also had to deal with the threat of deployment that never quite disappeared. Deployments mean separation as well as the ongoing uncertainty and concern that the service member might not come home. This was difficult to ignore.

As much as I, at times, disliked the military because of the ongoing uncertainty, I also always felt at home. The military was a kind of family and, strangely, gave me a sense of belonging. My husband did not feel the same. He left the military around 2000 because he could no longer tolerate the environment. I continued with my studies at UTSA, majoring in psychology and completing my premed requirements to keep my career options open. My professors encouraged me to pursue my dreams and aspirations. At the time I attended UTSA, it was a much smaller university than it is today. I recall walking into all my professors' offices without appointments, just to chat; these were opportunities to explore and broaden my interests and perspective. UTSA was a place to learn and to grow, far away from the realities of life.

Then September 11, 2001 came, and everything changed. As I am writing this, it has been twelve years since that life-changing day. I was stuck in an organic chemistry lab at the time, and our instructor would not allow us to leave until the class had concluded. By the time we left, the events were unfolding on TVs that had been put up around campus. With sheer terror and disbelief, students just stared; some were angry, some cried, and everyone hurt. It was an eerie day. I recall just sitting in the hallway in the psychology department crying.

I was twenty-three years old. Like many young people, I wanted to go; I wanted to make things right. Of course, there was no recourse for me to do so at that time. I talked to my family, to friends, to strangers. I waited, like so many others, for hours to give blood. What else could I do? Nothing. Feeling powerless and helpless was not a good feeling.

Like most Americans, I followed events closely. Over the next few days, weeks, months, and, eventually, years, I saw our military deploy. I read about our casualties and those missing in action. I thought of the service members being deployed and the families who had to live without their loved ones, often for months, if not years. I thought of the wives, husbands, and children left behind—of their pain, their fear, and their agony when they received a notification stating that he or she was not coming home. I thought of how I had felt several years earlier when my first husband (who was then my boyfriend) had deployed to Saudi Arabia and I had heard on the radio that there had been a bombing in Dhahran. I have known this fear, but I was spared the bad news that he had been hurt or killed.

My helplessness turned into frustration, frustration into determination, and determination into action. There was nothing I could do at that moment; however, I had choices about the future, and I would consider them wisely. Somehow, some way, I would make my contribution.

As luck would have it, during my senior year in college, I met the person who later would commission me as a Naval Officer in 2011. His name was Jim Startin, a retired Air Force colonel with a lovely wife. I became friends with both of them. Colonel Startin encouraged me to pursue my goal of joining the military.

In the spring of 2003, I graduated summa cum laude with a BA in psychology from UTSA. However, uncertain of whether I wanted to pursue an MD, a PhD, or both, I decided to stay one additional year at UTSA to complete more classes. In the end, I decided to attend a PhD program in physiology at Dartmouth, in part because I needed to get out of a failing marriage and in part because it was a terrific program and a great opportunity. My decision, however, left me restless. After a year in the program, I realized that psychology is where I belonged, and I started to reapply to graduate programs in clinical psychology.

ORANGE AND WHITE

Throughout all the changes—the move from Texas to New Hampshire, starting graduate school, reapplying to graduate school—I also went through a rather stressful divorce. I was fortunate to meet my second husband, a Sailor, shortly after. Cody was a K-9 MA (Master at Arms) in the Navy, and initially we were literally dating across the continent. My husband enjoyed the Navy, but his true passion was, and continues to be, law enforcement. He decided to leave the Navy once his four-year contract was up and relocate to New Hampshire to be with me. He was supportive of my decision to leave the program in physiology and pursue a graduate degree in psychology instead. I was accepted at the UT Austin clinical psychology program, the one I had always dreamed of. In the summer of 2006, we returned to Austin to start a new life in my favorite city and my top-choice program.

The clinical psychology program at UT Austin is challenging. While the program emphasizes research skills, it also intends to train highly competent clinicians. Although it is the goal of the program to see its graduates join faculties at renowned universities, some of us end up choosing clinical careers. At UT, I had wonderful mentors as well as terrific colleagues, and many of them turned into friends.

During the third year at UT, students are required to choose practicum placements, and my top choice was the nearby Department of Veterans Affairs (VA). I was matched with the site and remained there for three years. The veterans and their families gave me a glimpse into the lives of service members following deployments to Iraq and Afghanistan. They made their sacrifices and the toll it had taken on them, as well as their families, crystal clear.

I learned about their ongoing struggles, including those associated with returning to college—something that someone like me, who had spent most of her life in school, initially found difficult to comprehend. After all, these young men and women had gone to war, had to live in dire conditions and in constant danger. How could college pose a challenge?

The more I worked with my veterans, the more I understood. Some did not like the confinement of the classroom; some were frequently distracted and in general had a hard time concentrating; some hated the questions asked by other students who had not been in the military, the most frequent and irritating of which were, "Dude, have you ever killed anyone? What was it like?" And seemingly all of the veterans seemed to dread the crowds associated with college campuses.

Many of these brave young men and women who had joined the military came back having seen things that most adults would struggle to deal with. Many had been involved in unimaginable experiences. My patients struggled to cope with their experiences, but they had been brave once again to seek help for their difficulties and were determined to get better.

At times I felt like a phony, working with veterans without yet having served myself. Do not misunderstand: the majority of clinicians at the VA do not have military experience; they are excellent clinicians who do a phenomenal job. I also do not believe that in order to treat disorders (e.g., Post-Traumatic Stress Disorder, or PTSD) one has to have been diagnosed with it; to me, this is similar to saying that in order to treat cancer you should be a cancer survivor.

The past had caught up with me, and once again, I asked the question, "What could I do?" So, one day while at the VA (I believe I was in my fourth year of graduate school at the time), I tried to get in touch with the medical recruiter via the Navy's website. It took me two months following the initial call to finally get the right name and receive a call back. I could have given up, I could have said this is too much work, but I didn't.

For nearly two years, I worked with this recruiter to allow me to apply to the Navy Clinical Psychology internship. My recruiter, himself a novice at recruiting psychology graduate students, was exceptional and professional. He presented the facts as much as he could and always answered my questions. He was my first encounter with the "Navy Chief" and in my opinion an example of what a Navy Chief should be.

Meanwhile, some of my colleagues, as well as faculty members, were slightly disconcerted by the fact that I had considered putting myself in harm's way. While I was excited and hopeful to deploy quickly after internship (although I was aware that licensure had to be completed prior to any deployment), some of them appeared to be horrified. I started to realize that not everyone shared my enthusiasm for the military, let alone for deployment. However, my path was set—for the most part. I will spare the reader the details of the lengthy application process that included seemingly endless paperwork, interminable waiting, and my first brush with the military's "hurry up and wait" philosophy.

I had not made this decision lightly, nor without consulting with those who were in charge of this training. I consulted with the internship director in San Diego, Dr. Mather, about the internship as well as the Navy. Dr. Mather, a retired Navy captain, turned out to be not only an incredibly intelligent individual, but also one of the funniest and kindhearted people I have met. If he is reading this, I am sure he will make a rather "fitting" comment; it didn't hurt that he also was a UT football fan. The interview with him was delightful and interesting.

The weeks leading up to finding out where I had "matched" (i.e., which internship I would eventually attend) were long. I had ranked the Navy as my number one choice because I wanted to work with this population, and I wanted to walk the walk. While I have great respect for the men and women working in the VA, some of whom are veterans themselves, it was not enough to just work with them. I wanted to share this experience with them, and after eleven years of training, I finally had the chance to do just that in the profession that I had chosen. Of course, there are always sacrifices: if I matched with this internship, I would not be able to pursue my immediate aspiration of becoming a neuropsychologist. In fact, I would not be able to administer any of the tests I had previously come to know and love. However, the sacrifice appeared worth it.

When I received the call that I had matched with the clinical psychology internship in San Diego, I was not that surprised. I had a strong application and a background fitting the training environment. My supportive husband was happy for us, although this would mean geographic separation for several years. Nevertheless, we would make it work—like we always had. During the spring semester I worked hard on my dissertation, frantically trying to finish at least my results section so I would be able to attend Officer Development School (ODS) unburdened. While my colleagues celebrated their last summer in Austin prior to their departure or were eagerly settling into their internships throughout the country, I had the pleasure of attending "boot camp for officers" in Newport, Rhode Island.

BLUE AND GOLD

I was commissioned by my friend and retired Colonel Startin on a lovely day in June of 2011. Several weeks later—on July 15, 2011 to be exact—I arrived in Providence, Rhode Island. I took a cab with several other officers I had met at the airport to Newport. Newport is a rather expensive yet beautiful little town in New England that offers beautiful scenery and amazing seafood. It is also the place where naval officers are trained. Newport's community is very supportive of the Navy; it is not unusual to be told "thank you for your service" or even to have a stranger pay for your dinner.

Arriving at ODS was like stepping into a twilight zone. Small rooms held a desk and a locker that were supposed to be kept clean and identical; if they weren't, everyone would get in trouble. In addition to ODS, Newport is also the home of several other programs, including Officer Candidate School (OCS). Unlike ODS students who attend ODS as already-commissioned naval officers, OCS students still have to earn their commission. Also, while ODS is five weeks long, OCS requires twelve weeks of training. Because ODS is considered easy, it has received several nicknames, such as "fork and knife school" and "bad summer camp."

The truth is, looking back, it was the experience of a lifetime. I met some amazing people and had some unusual experiences, such as firefighting and trying to keep a sinking ship afloat (the USS Buttercup). The five weeks passed faster than expected, in part because I was constantly sleep-deprived while trying my best to be in charge of forty-one people. Frankly, sometimes I failed; actually, *many* times I failed. But that was part of it. I was grateful for the experience, for the camaraderie, and for the sense of togetherness. I graduated ODS on August 19, 2011 and was sent to the Naval Medical Center in San Diego to start my internship. There I would reunite with five officers with whom I had graduated from ODS.

Life as a psychology intern is in general stressful—you are considered a clinician and have to manage your time well. Many interns complete their dissertations during internship, further adding to the already busy schedule of managing patient care (with supervision), report writing, and record keeping. However, in a military internship, it is equally important to learn to be a Naval officer and to learn the unique challenges and regulations associated with Navy medicine. In addition, every sailor is expected to maintain physical fitness and weight standards. To say that I was busy is an understatement, but, taken in perspective, the Navy offered me the opportunity I had been waiting for: to work with active-duty service members and to become part of their community.

During my internship, I worked at multiple sites, including the Marine Corps Recruit Depot and Fleet Mental Health, and in several areas, including health psychology, inpatient, and adult outpatient care. Each rotation offered me different opportunities and perspectives along with different challenges. In addition, as part of my particular corps requirement, I served as a Medical Service Corps Officer. I had to stand Officer of the Day (OOD) watch about every forty-five days. That meant that after 4:00 pm, once the Commanding Officer had left the hospital, I was the main contact to authorize after-hour repairs, deal with emergencies, and even "sign in" individuals who were in the brig and had to be treated at NMCSD.

This job was very different from everything I had done in my life, but, once again, I had great support from my community, who would look out for me when I had questions or concerns. I felt truly fortunate to be amongst those sailors. Although tasks such as standing watch are critical and mission important, and we were all busy and took these tasks seriously, we also retained a good sense of humor. One Friday, I was in the unfortunate position of ending up with four cell phones: my personal cell phone, my command cell phone, my consult liaison cell phone, and my OOD cell phone. In addition, another officer who had just checked into the command was standing a break in watch with me. A break in watch means that you have another officer tag along so that he or she gets an idea about the job as an OOD; this is part of the qualification process to become watch qualified.

At 4:00 pm, I was supposed to attend a staff meeting to ensure that I was aware of any ongoing issues on the hospital wards. Well, it just so happened that on my way to the meeting, all four phones rang simultaneously. I picked up my OOD phone first, and on the other end of the line I heard "Sorry, wrong number." Bad mistake, because I immediately recognized my friend Dave's voice, and it dawned on me what just had happened: four of my colleagues (Dave, Ann, Allison, and Manny) had all decided to try to give me a heart attack by calling all of my phones at the same time. They almost succeeded. It was one of the best pranks, and one I will never forget.

In March 2012, we all received orders to our new duty stations. I was asked to reconsider my first choice and select a location that would require a rather independent graduate who needed little supervision. I agreed to take the orders to Naval Hospital Pensacola. However, prior to arriving at my first official duty station, I was fortunate to be the first Naval psychology intern to complete survival school, aka SERE (Survival, Evade, Resist, Escape) school. In part, my request was approved because I would be working at an aviation command; the truth is that several rates or MOSs (military specialty occupations) require completion of survival school, and I believed that volunteering for challenging schools and training would give me some "street cred" at my new command and beyond. It was a challenging two weeks of training, but it was also some of the best training I have ever received.

PENSACOLA AND BEYOND

I am currently stationed in Pensacola. For the most part, I work with Marine and Navy students who are straight out of boot camp and are in Pensacola to complete their A-school (i.e., they are here to learn the job they will have in the military). The transition into the military can be challenging, and in part it is my job to help young sailors and Marines adjust to the military. Of course, most students do not come to see us and have no problems adjusting to the military, but we provide services for the small percentage that do.

One of the most frequent statements I hear when I ask students what they are planning to do following their service is, "I will return to college;" when I ask what is better about college, the typical answer is, "freedom—I can do what I want." For someone who has spent the better part of twelve years in college and graduate school, this statement is a little unsettling. Personally, I believe that college is not necessarily an easier route. The challenges are different, and some of these students would do well to complete four years of military service in order to acquire the discipline necessary to become successful college students. The military has a lot to offer, and typically students are taken care of, especially while they are in school: they are provided with food, a room, and structure that many have not had before. They get paid well, especially for eighteen-year-olds straight out of high school, and they also earn money for a college education.

GIVEN THE CHOICE AND WOMEN IN THE MILITARY

Recently, one of my fellow graduate students contacted me because she was interested in choosing the same path that I have. She asked me if I thought I had made the right decision. This gave me an opportunity to reflect on my decision. I certainly missed my opportunity to complete a neuropsychology fellowship; this is quite difficult for me. However, military service is always tied to sacrifice; this is likely even more true of women in the military. At some point, we have to decide if we want to serve or have a family, or if we are able to combine the two in some way. Many marriages have dissolved because husbands were unhappy with the frequent deployments and moves and not being able to have a career or a life. While this is a fact of life for so many female spouses, it is not necessarily the case for military husbands. And although times are changing, it remains true that most support groups were created for female spouses.

As for me, the separation and the stress associated with my job became too much for my second marriage. It is challenging to be married to someone in the military, and currently I find myself in dual roles as both an active duty service member and the girlfriend of an active duty service member. It is interesting to be on both sides concurrently and having to balance the stresses associated with each. Looking back, there are certainly things I would have done differently. Then again, I can't do anything about my past decisions, but I certainly can influence my future.

DISCLAIMER

The views expressed in this article are those of the author(s) and do not necessarily reflect the official policy or position of the Department of the Navy, Department of Defense, or the United States Government.

COPYRIGHT

DAVID WEBER
COAST GUARD

David was an undergraduate student back when I was an adjunct faculty member at UTSA. In the ensuing twenty years, we have both raised families and continued our academic journeys. He has since obtained both his BA and MA, and he is now a PhD candidate in the Psychology Graduate Program at UTSA, which has an emphasis on Military Health. As a Coast Guard veteran and a keen intellectual, David brings a unique viewpoint to discussions of both military service and academics.

The Nix. I was born at the Nix Hospital, as legend has it, a week early and just in time for a New Year's Eve party. I think my parents had planned to ring out 1963 with a bang and ring in 1964 with a new baby. I, however, had other plans. It seems the Christmas party was so much fun I didn't want to miss the festivities surrounding the New Year. This did not stop my parents.

Parties in one form or another have always been an integral part of my family's dynamic. I suppose that may have something to do with my parents being part of the WWII generation. Both being born in the twenties and in an agrarian society, the Great Depression was less a calamity than simply the way life was. So when any reason to have some fun was heard of, found, or invented, it was enthusiastically pursued. Now, to be sure, my parents and all of their families, friends, and neighbors all worked hard from daylight to dusk; there is always a lot to do on a farm. However, that only seemed to have emphasized how much fun having fun actually was.

With the onset of WWII, the reasons, as well as the ability, to go carousing were greatly curtailed, but that did not deaden or lessen the positive attitude toward engaging in good, clean fun. On the contrary: the hardships suffered by the civilian and military populations, along with the victorious conclusion of WWII, seemed to have enhanced the desire to celebrate something and everything. So, with five children (I was fourth out of five), that's seven birthdays, four major holidays, six minor holidays, plus the random wedding or spontaneous gathering, so we had plenty of reasons to party.

I did not like school. It was something I was supposed to do. Work is also something you're supposed to do. Work is not fun. Work is to be endured and suffered through so that you can then have fun. School may not have been work, but it was too close to it to be fun. I did learn stuff, though, and I made fair to middling grades. All my friends were at school, but still it just did not seem like a very fun place to me.

Academics in general were not fun. I could not read effectively until well into my grade school years. As a child, if I needed to read anything, I would find an older sibling to read it to me, or I would just study any pictures associated with the story and figure it out. I did, however, look through the World Book Encyclopedia every night. I knew every page, from A to Z and even the yearly synopsis. I didn't read anything, but I memorized every picture in the collection. I never read a book cover to cover until after I had graduated high school. I tried a couple of times, but I just lost interest. I still have issues with reading, although I have read many, many things in the years since then, and I read very slowly for an academic. Science and math were really the only reasons my grades did not fail me out. Those subjects were fun, but I didn't allow myself the luxury of liking them.

After high school, I enrolled at UTSA in 1981, but dropped out because my grades were not good enough to pass. The environment at the university was very different from high school.

In high school, the expectation was that you went to class, and if you didn't, quite often your parents knew before the school did. My father made it very clear that if I wasn't going to go to school, I *would* be going to work in the field. Hence, I was in class every day.

In college, though, no one really cared if I went to class. I was expected to be a college student, but after that, all the pressure to actually attend class was gone, so the natural course of events was to exercise my newfound independence. Of course, this led to the necessity of having to drop out.

Dropping out of college had a rather sobering consequence. I was aware of the theoretic possibility and intellectually understood the high likelihood of this situation actually coming to pass, but the reality was … shocking, to say the least. I had no place to live. My parents made good on their stipulation that I could live at home only as long as I was furthering my education. Having left school, my home was no longer where I was welcome to stay.

At seventeen, I was faced with some serious life choices and few good options. In assessing the situation, I identified three basic needs: food, clothing, and shelter. Applying my meager income from working construction to this needs matrix demonstrated to me that I could cover the first two, but shelter was going to be a bit tricky. Facing such a bleak dilemma, coupled with a limited employment landscape, the easiest and most obvious choice for me was the military. Since is also offered the stability of a steady paycheck, it was a no-brainer. Deciding on which branch to join was the next hurdle.

I guess I should explain that someone in my extended family has been in the military during every major conflict since 1844, with the possible exception of the Mexican-American war of 1846–1848. My great-grandfather was in the Civil War, my father and uncles were in WWII, and I have had cousins in the Spanish-American War, WWII, Korea, Vietnam, and Iraq. To be sure, not everyone in my family has been part of the military, and, in actuality, the number of military servicemen in my family is small compared to the total. It is, however, recognized as an honorable endeavor, so a stint in the armed forces had always been on the table as a career choice.

Back in the late '70s and early '80s, the big four had recruiters everywhere. They came to the high schools, and all the upper class male students took the Armed Services Vocational Aptitude Battery (ASVAB), so awareness of the Army, Navy, Air Force, and Marines was not an issue, nor was my initial decision about which one to join. The Marines seemed too hard-core, the Air Force seemed too high and mighty, and the Army was too ground oriented, but the Navy had big ships that went to different and exotic places, and I liked salt water. Hence, the Navy seemed like the direction I needed to go.

I think a brief word needs to be said about military recruiters. I know the military needs recruiters. I know they have a thankless job. I know they go to a number of schools to learn their jobs—which forms to fill out, what skills to look for, and how best to fill the ranks with the best and brightest. I also know they have certain expectations as to how many persons should be processed through their offices each year, although quota may be too strong a word. Still, them some lyin' bastards. I have never met another military service member who said their recruiter told the truth. Now, saying they outright lie may be a bit harsh; however, the rosy picture painted by the recruiter never seems to materialize. So, a word to the wise: be wary of smiling strangers bearing contracts.

My personal experience was slightly less disappointing. The Navy recruiter was nice. He was very excited when he saw my ASVAB scores. He promised me all kinds of schooling possibilities. He said boot camp was not as bad as the stories say. He said for someone like me, advancement was an easy stair-step to success. All I needed to do was sign on the dotted line. He met my parents (my dad kinda looked at him a little sideways) and promised them the Navy was the place for me. Everyone was very optimistic and impressed.

People have never called me "dumb." They have used many other words to describe me, but never the word "dumb." I told the recruiter that I had reviewed the other services and decided to sign up with the Navy. The only sticking point was that I had not been able to locate a Coast Guard recruiter. My father, you see, had served in the Coast Guard during WWII, and in deference to him, I thought I should at least see what they had to offer, so I asked the Navy recruiter to get me in touch with them. My idea was that the Navy should have nothing to worry about from the Coast Guard and I could demonstrate to my dad and to myself that I had investigated all my options. In addition, this would give me one more example of the spotless integrity of the Navy recruiter. It must have been as difficult for the recruiter to find the Coast Guard recruiting office as it was for me, because he never could locate the phone number for their San Antonio office.

From time to time, circumstances have arisen that have had a fortuitous influence upon the direction of my life. It just so happened that, while all this was going on, a high school buddy of mine who had joined the Navy straight out of school came home for a visit. One day we were talking about the Navy and what I should expect (his stories seemed a lot different from the recruiters') and I told him I was waiting to talk to the Coast Guard, but that there was some difficulty in locating a recruiter office.

He said, "Let's go find one."

I said, "Where are we going to look?"

He said, "There should be one downtown with all the other military main offices."

I said, "Ok, let's go."

Oddly enough, the Coast Guard's recruiting office was right next door to the Navy's, in the same building. I had never been to these specific offices, and I assume the Navy recruiter hadn't, either. So my buddy and I went in and looked around. It was a rather bare-bones office—just a smallish reception room, an adjacent room for private consultations, and a private office in the back. The only real advertisements for the service were posters on the walls—pictures of buoy tenders, cutters on calm seas, helicopters hovering over a rescue scene—but what caught my attention was the picture of a 44-ft. rescue boat surfing a huge wave.

When the Coast Guard recruiter came in, he asked how he could help us. I pointed to the picture and asked, "Could I do that?" He looked at me kind of funny and asked who I was. I then commenced to tell him the story about the Navy and me. He said he could not promise me any of the things the Navy recruiter had and that there was no guarantee that I would get to a station where those rescue boats were used. I asked him about boot camp, and he told me some ugly stories about it, but that it wasn't as bad as what the Marines go through. I asked him about chipping paint and scrubbing barnacles off of buoys (my father had mentioned this). He laughed and nodded his head yes. So I asked, "Where do I sign?" and started the best time of my life.

Boot camp for the Coast Guard is in Cape May, New Jersey. It was a lot of fun *getting* to boot camp—flying into Pittsburgh and then the bus ride to Cape May—but the fun pretty much stopped when the bus did.

Boot camp was not fun. However, I did learn a lot about myself. Like how far I could run before I threw up. How many pushups I could do before my arms started to shake, violently. How much sleep I did not need. I also learned there were other people from other places besides San Antonio and that they were not very different from myself (well, some were). A neat thing I learned was that I could keep my wisdom teeth (still have them) and that I got better at running, pushups, and not sleeping. It still was not fun.

At the completion of boot camp, I was given three options: go to Corpus Christi, TX, to Guam, or to a place in Alaska called Ketchikan. Since I'm from Texas and wanted to see other things, I chose Alaska (Guam seemed a bit too exotic and far away for my poor constitution at the time). I also got to go home for ten whole days before I had to report to my new duty station.

My triumphant return from boot camp was a little disappointing. It seemed nobody really realized I had left. People did wonder where I had disappeared to, but no one missed me. Moreover, all of my boot camp stories seemed to generate laughter but not much interest. So when I flew out for Alaska I was a little disappointed. My first impression of Alaska was little better.

It was raining when I landed in Seattle. It was raining when I left Seattle thirty minutes later. It was raining when I landed in Ketchikan. It rained on me for the next six months. Those 180 days were pretty miserable. There were some good things that happened, and I met some good people. Daddy always told me the first friends you make are a cook and a quartermaster. The first one will see to it that you get fed; the other will make sure you get paid. This turned out to be very good advice.

I was also assigned to the Search and Rescue department of the support base called the SAR locker. We ran two small boats: a 41-ft. patrol boat and a 44-ft. foul-weather rescue boat, the same type I saw on the poster in the recruiter's office. Nevertheless, as often happens, with the good comes the bad.

I suppose the worst (and maybe the best) thing that happened to me was a First Class Boatswains mate who simply detested the fact that I was in his Coast Guard. To state that he woke up every morning just to ruin my day would be a classic understatement, and for those first several months he was quite successful. Not only did I not do anything right, if I did (somehow by accident), something from the previous day or previous week would be shown as evidence that I was simply the poorest excuse for a Coasty. I was at a pretty low state, and it must have been pretty obvious, because the Chief pulled me off to the side and advised me that I should put in for some vacation time. He said he would authorize some advancement of extra leave time, so I went home.

This time my homecoming was very different; I was actually missed. I think I was there for around twelve days, and it was one long celebration. It gave me a sense of being important to someone.

MICHAEL SMITH
AIR FORCE

Michael is an insightful young man who recently got engaged, works in the Student Disabilities office on campus, and served in the Military Police while deployed in the Middle East. Despite the intensity of his wartime experiences, he exhibits maturity beyond his years and a genuine concern for others. The first time I spoke with him, he came up to me after class to inquire about how he could help a fellow military member who was experiencing difficulty adjusting to civilian life.

From an early age, I was taught that a formal education is not only handy in society, but it can also be exceptionally meaningful at the individual level. Growing up with this mindset helped me propel myself through the rigors of education and even the military itself. Although I did not do well academically in elementary or even middle school, I found a passion in college, not only for the education itself, but also for the institution of learning. I found myself drawn to the open-mindedness common on college campuses around the world. This was especially true since I was coming from a world of strict regulations, customs, and conventions about what people could and couldn't say. Once in college, I found myself drawn into deep conversations with my peers about the meaning of everything, including religion, life, and even the military itself. This was certainly an eye-opening and exciting experience for me.

I was raised by my father for much of my childhood, and was fortunate in that he supported all of my ideas about self-growth. However, he was a retired professor in special education, and he was not thrilled by the idea of my joining the military during wartime, especially during an unpopular and questionable war. As a result, I found myself trying to subdue his hesitation with claims of adventure, independence, and educational possibilities. At that time, my decisions were strongly influenced by the propaganda surrounding war, which has been much the same throughout history. In my position as a Military Police Member (Security Forces), I quickly learned that my expectations about the experience and the reality of what it is differ greatly.

My expectation for my deployment in Iraq was that I would help the Iraqi people develop a new and stable government, as well as helping them provide security for their country and countrymen. Of course, this was not the case. I was assigned to Detainee Operations in one of the largest detainee facilities in the Middle East. My deployment was extremely simple and safe compared to many other units that were deployed in Iraq from 2006 to 2007.

Most of the violence within the detainment facility was directed towards other detainees, and was mainly based on religious differences between the Sunnis and Shiites. Again, this was unexpected. I did not expect to see so many young boys under the age of eighteen and old men above the age of sixty-five at the detainment facility, or detained in general. It was not my job to judge them or their actions, and I do believe many of the detainees did deserve to be there, but many did not. Every single detainee I spoke with wanted and demanded a trial. Many had been waiting for over three years for a trial or even to have a formal charge filed against them.

During my enlistment, and especially after my deployment, I learned how to adapt to the structure, general lifestyle, and unwritten rules of the military. Simply asking for an accommodating schedule to use educational benefits was seen as comical and was downright ignored. I quickly understood that I would not have enough time in between shifts to take classes, even if they were available. I learned quickly that this was the nature of the beast that is the military.

My time in the military taught me—as well as many others before and after me—discipline, time management, and procedural processing; everything had an order to it.

Those facets help me greatly today in my pursuit of higher education. While the thought of studying and completing certain assignments would have intimidated me in the past, today I am able to break down those tasks procedurally, analyze them, and approach them differently. This has allowed me to excel greatly among my peers, both in and outside of the military. Essentially, by using the same tactics I learned in the military, I have been able to prioritize tasks and motivate myself to complete those readings/assignments as though it was a "sink or swim/ do or die" situation. The discipline and self-restraint that I have learned through the military has helped me succeed, academically and in many other aspects.

As a result of my military experiences, I have decided that I would like to pursue a career helping my fellow veterans as they transition into college. Here at the University of Texas at San Antonio, the Veterans Certification Office was extremely helpful in making my adjustment to university life a success. The office explained the procedures and expectations that I would have to adhere to, which I found comforting; responsibility was always an integral feature of the military lifestyle and culture. One has a responsibility not only for themselves, but also for the friend or comrade next to them. There is always someone along the chain of command who will hold you accountable for all your actions, and I accepted this mindset quickly. I learned that excuses were not permitted nor encouraged in the military, especially during deployment. Your life, as well as the lives of others, was literally and figuratively in your hands.

In college, this translated into my taking full responsibility for the specific scores or marks I received. Although I am still ambivalent about some aspects of my time in the military, I am also extremely grateful for the skills and mindset that the military has taught me, which in turn has enabled me to pursue my aspirations and discover my future.

TIFFANY MENDOZA
AIR FORCE

Tiffany's quick laugh and ready smile disguise her struggles to become one of the first people in her family to obtain a college degree. Whether working in the restaurant business until all hours of the night, volunteering to go back overseas, or supporting the members of her family, Tiffany's optimism and compassion are an integral component of her character and her coping.

I was a member of the Air Force ROTC in high school, and I liked it enough to decide that if I ever joined the military, this would be the branch for me. After graduating, I went straight to Texas Tech, and my boyfriend at the time and I went to see a recruiter. This turned out to be funny, because he was disqualified and I just sort of enlisted when I realized that they would pay for school.

I was active duty from 2003–2010, and was deployed in 2007, 2008, and 2009. The day after my active duty contract was up, I enlisted in the Air National Guard, but I have found the transition difficult. I miss the camaraderie of my military units, and would like to be given more responsibility. I am currently looking to get commissioned by the Air Force, or even the Army, so I can continue on to law school.

As soon as I completed my technical training with the Air Force, I was allowed to take college courses, and found my units extremely helpful. The classes I took during my active service were free, and I had funding for three more years of school after my contract was up. This has allowed me to complete my BA without any student debt. I know that the Hazelwood Act will give me another 120 hours of free school, too. The military has been great to me, and I am happy to be a veteran.

WILLIAM MCMILLEN
ARMY

William is in turn a soldier, student, veteran, husband of an active- duty service member and a father. Despite the complexity of these roles, he moves between them with a quick smile, and a positive outlook. During my Stress Management class I found myself looking forward to his witty, insightful comments, as did the rest of the class. On one memorable occasion, he emailed me to say that he thought his wife was in labor so he would need to take a rain check on our lab meeting. Needless to say, I accepted his excuse.

TRANSITION: FROM CIVILIAN TO SOLDIER AND BACK AGAIN

To become a civilian again after being a soldier can be a long and confusing process. The same can be said for becoming a soldier after being a civilian. I have gone through the process several times and have learned a few things along the way. I joined the active duty Army on the 25th of May, 2003. This first period of active duty service lasted until August of 2008. I went back to being a civilian, but only for a year before I decided to apply for Army Officer Candidate School.

On August 20th of 2009, I arrived in Fort Benning, Georgia to attend and conquer this new task. After serving over three years as an active duty officer in the Army, I decided to leave active duty again, and ended up joining the National Guard. I only stayed for about a year, and I am now no longer serving in the military in any capacity. Why did I go back and forth? I'm not exactly sure myself.

The military is a simple organization once you understand how it works, but it completely changes your life. I was a longhaired, guitar-playing pacifist in my former civilian life before committing myself to the military. I was changed into a shorthaired, gun-toting man of action, ready to accomplish whatever was thrown at me.

I was instilled with discipline by waking up at 0430 every morning, shaving, and then running five miles before the sun came up. I received training that would give me the confidence to take on any challenge without fear and conquer all self-doubt. I was given a weapon and equipment, then taught how to use and care for it all. I learned how to take a weapon apart and put it back together, along with how to clean it and make sure that it was in proper working condition. I was given responsibility and expected to produce results. I was broken down in order to be built up into a new person, and it has never left me.

After all the training was complete, I was sent to my first unit, and after some more training I was deployed to Iraq. Military training changes you, but it doesn't stop there. Deploying to a foreign country charged with the responsibility of representing your country's strength and values is something not many people experience (In the US, less than 1 percent). Wearing the uniform makes you a symbol. Your actions aren't just yours alone anymore; they are also the actions of the US as a whole. Whatever you do, however you act, will be a direct reflection on your country and may be the only impression any foreigners get of the US. It was a very important thing with which to be entrusted, but we were prepared to do so. There are many more stories I could share, many other examples, but I think I have proven the point that becoming a soldier is a life-changing process.

Many people leave the military for many different reasons, but ultimately all must leave someday and become civilians again. The first thing to go is the uniform, and with it the respect that it brings to the person wearing it. I have lost count of the times I was thanked for my service, given a free meal, or upgraded to first class on a plane, all because I was wearing my military uniform. The people who offered all of these things didn't know who I was and might not have offered anything if they did. They just knew that I was a US Army soldier, and thus showed respect and kindness for it.

Along with the uniform and respect goes the responsibility and authority. In the military, a person is responsible for others and to others. Everyone is both a supervisor and a subordinate to someone else, and as such everyone is responsible for each other in some way. It is a very structured system and everyone knows their place, but once you leave the military, this structure is no longer valid.

During my year as a civilian before becoming a military officer, I worked as a compliance manager at a construction company. I didn't start off in that position, but rather as an assistant. I always kept the manager informed: I would tell her what I was working on and when I was stepping out for a bathroom break or for coffee. One day, she said, "Why do you always tell me when you are leaving?" I was confused until it dawned on me how different the military was from the civilian sector. She wasn't my superior the way I had them in the military. She didn't outrank me, she just out earned me. I eventually became the manager because people came to me for compliance issues just as often, or more, than the managers. I started signing off my e-mails as the "Compliance Manager," and thus the title became mine. I could have never just assumed somebody's role in the military, but in that company, nobody batted an eye when I did exactly that.

Finally, a soldier gives up being a symbol and a part of something whose tradition is bigger than anything they can ever expect to be a part of again. It is very improbable that, as a civilian, you will ever take part in a parade or ceremony honoring the sacrifices of the employees you work with or their great past traditions. I can say with almost absolute certainty that as a civilian you will never have ceremonies where cannons and rifles are fired, parachutists are jumping from planes, or large masses of coworkers are running together in order to honor the work you are doing. There is nowhere else in society where these traditions occur. For people outside of the military, it is very hard to fully grasp what they mean and why we do them.

So what is left now? A civilian who was once a soldier and memories of what now seems like a past life. Now all that experience is put down on a resume and handed to a hiring manager who looks at your military experience like it's written in a foreign language. They can see that you've "handled millions of dollars' worth of equipment" and "supervised twenty personnel in a high-stress, results-oriented environment." They can see that you are accustomed to working twelve-hour shifts for fifteen months straight with no weekends, and it confuses the hell out of them. Translating military skills and experience into a normal 9-to-5 job can be more stressful and intimidating than a deployment to a warzone.

Most people who have served at least one term in the military are competent people with a solid work ethic and an amazing amount of attention to detail, yet, according to the Bureau of Labor Statistics, the unemployment rate for veterans who served from September 2001 to the present was 9 percent in 2013. Some of this can be attributed to having to start a new career or attend school, and still more can be attributed to a general misunderstanding of the skills that a veteran can bring to an organization.

A veteran is dedicated to organizational goals and will go the extra mile (literally with a rucksack if needed) to get the job done. A veteran is used to getting up early, being on time, and not calling in sick. A veteran has probably had to make some hard decisions and is used to working in teams. The one disadvantage a veteran might have is that many don't want to shine a light on their accomplishments and don't want to stand apart from the group. Veterans are used to being part of a well-oiled machine that accomplishes big things without saying, "look at me." Nobody likes a show-off, but in the private sector a person has to toot his own horn sometimes, and this can be a problem for many vets who are used to having a silent sense of pride.

The problems for the veteran are not insurmountable, but they are difficult. I hope that I have shed some light on these difficulties so that future veteran employers, coworkers, and veterans themselves can think about them and work together to find solutions. Leaving your job can be tough, but leaving an entire culture that molded you and a close circle of friends who endured hardship with you can be downright paralyzing. It takes a while to recover from the loss of support and to find stable footing in a strange new world. My hope is that we as a society of both veterans and civilians can find a way together that benefits everyone.

JOHN LIRA
MARINES

When she heard that I was editing a book on veteran student experiences at UTSA, Dr. Ann Eisenberg, the Interim Dean of the Honors College, suggested that I contact John about writing a chapter. By that time, John was already attending graduate school, having finished his degree at UTSA in a blaze of honors and awards. Fortunately, he graciously agreed to take time from his studies and family life to write about his military and academic experiences.

At the age of seventeen, I made the most consequential commitment of my life when I raised my right hand and repeated the Armed Forces Oath of Enlistment to become a United States Marine. The thought of becoming a Marine allowed me to imagine an entirely new life of opportunity and service. I graduated from Marine basic training only five months after graduating from high school, marking the second major accomplishment of my adult life.

Becoming a Marine fundamentally changed me from a high school kid into a well-trained and disciplined soldier. While on active duty, I worked as a satellite communications operator. My duty stations included Okinawa, Japan and Camp Pendleton, California. At the age of twenty-one, I was among the first US combat forces to cross from Kuwait into Iraq with the First Marine Division in what would ultimately be called Operation Iraqi Freedom.

Shortly after my return from Iraq, my active duty enlistment expired and I returned to San Antonio, where I joined the local Marine Reserve unit as an Intelligence Analyst. During this time, I also used my GI Bill benefits to enroll as a full-time student at San Antonio College (SAC). I really enjoyed being a student, but there were many difficulties I had to overcome. For example, the nature of my work in the Marines was restricted to the scope of my job function and did not require me to write or do mathematics. If I were to achieve academic success, I would have to familiarize myself with the basic principles of math and grammar. In the middle of my second semester at SAC, the drums of war began to sound.

In January of 2005, I prepared for my second tour to Iraq as a reservist with Fourth Reconnaissance Battalion. We were attached to Third Battalion Twenty-Fifth Marines out of Ohio, and began training for our perilous deployment to Al Anbar Province.

The atmosphere in Iraq had changed significantly in the year and a half since my first deployment. The threat of improvised explosive devices lurked around every corner. My battalion experienced casualties almost immediately upon arriving. Ultimately, forty-eight Marines, sailors, and interpreters from my battalion lost their lives in the desert sands of Iraq. The memories of this trying deployment still weigh heavily on my heart; however, there was a moment during the deployment when I experienced extreme joy and happiness. One day in August, the deadliest month in Iraq for my battalion, I received news that my wife had given birth to our daughter, Rozlyn. I had become a father in the middle of a combat zone.

After returning home from Iraq, I returned to San Antonio College to pursue a degree in Paralegal Studies. I chose this degree because the course focused on research and writing skills that would enhance the skill set I had developed as an Intelligence Analyst. I graduated from San Antonio College with an associate's degree, marking my first academic achievement.

After graduating from SAC, I wanted to continue my education, and I still had GI Bill benefits to use. In the fall of 2009, after completing a year of transfer credits at SAC, I transferred to the University of Texas at San Antonio (UTSA), where I chose to pursue a degree in political science because the coursework and research focused on topics relevant to the field of intelligence, such as international affairs and foreign policy. The transition from San Antonio College to UTSA was smooth: most of my credits transferred, and I had no problem working with UTSA's Veteran Certification Office to utilize my remaining GI Bill Benefits.

I joined the UTSA Honors College after my first semester. I welcomed the opportunity to enroll in courses of advanced rigor and research. I regard joining the Honors College as a game changer because it placed me in contact with some of the best advisors and administrators the university had to offer. I met two particular professors, Dr. Ann Eisenberg and Dr. Richard Gambitta, who played essential roles in developing both my academic resume and my ambition as an undergraduate. For the first time in my life, I had mentors who advised and guided my academic development. I came to depend on the trust, guidance, and support of both professors throughout my undergraduate experience, and most importantly, through the graduate application process.

Dr. Eisenberg is the Associate Dean of the UTSA Honors College. In my very first advising session, she began to lay out an academic plan that would enrich my academic experiences beyond my wildest expectations. Dr. Eisenberg recognized that my military experience, strong GPA, and interest in government made me a strong candidate for several public policy scholarships and fellowships, and she motivated me to apply to them.

I met Dr. Gambitta when I enrolled in his Constitutional Law course. I was intrigued by the subject matter of the class and his exceptional lecture style. I asked Dr. Gambitta to lead my honors thesis, which focused on Mexican drug trafficking organizations and the labels that define them.

As a college student, I managed to achieve an outstanding academic record. I joined the Student Veterans Association (SVA) on campus because it was the only student organization that focused on the academic success and special needs of the student veteran community. I served as Secretary of the SVA, helping to drive up membership and arranging guest speakers for our meetings.

I never considered attending graduate school until my junior year of college, when I was accepted to participate in two distinguished fellowship programs: the Public Policy and International Affairs (PPIA) Fellowship and the Bill Archer Fellowship. During the PPIA Fellowship at Princeton University, I was mentored by scholars and academics about the importance of quantitative scholarship and diversity in public leadership. My summer at Princeton's Woodrow Wilson School was academically challenging and professionally inspiring.

After PPIA, I spent a semester interning and studying in Washington, DC as a Bill Archer Fellow. I consider this experience my first scholarly deployment to the frontlines of American public policy. Both fellowship experiences combined to shift my desire to work in intelligence into a passion to become a leader in foreign policy.

After graduating from UTSA in May of 2012, I immediately began to assemble the most competitive graduate applications possible for six leading public policy schools. My graduate application was a culmination of my military service, professional work experience, and academic achievements. Ultimately, I accepted an offer to attend Carnegie Mellon University's H. John Heinz III College of Public Policy and Management. As a student, I continue to rely heavily on the fundamental characteristics that made me a good Marine. My early commitment to military service established a deeply rooted obligation to public service, specifically at the federal level.

MARK KASHIWABARA
ARMY

Raised on the laid-back beaches in Hawaii, Mark nevertheless adapted quickly to life in the military and went on to use his GI benefits to return to school. In spite of injuries, financial pressures, and academic stress, his infectious laugh made him a favorite of veteran and nonveteran students alike. Since leaving the military, he has gotten married, and is currently pursuing a master's degree in counseling at UTSA.

I was honorably discharged from the US Army in 2005 due to medical issues I acquired after deploying for Operation Iraqi Freedom. Although the end of my military career gave me the opportunity to pursue a college degree, doing so was not a new goal. The idea to get back into college was a part of me from the moment I first joined the military; I just did not realize that it would take so long.

As a veteran who saw combat and dealt with a lot more than most people my own age, I thought college life would be easy compared to what I had to endure all those years ago. After spending time in Kosovo in 1999 and Iraq in 2003, it seemed that college life should be a piece of cake. I was looking forward to pursuing a career that did not involve being shot at by rocket-propelled grenades, having to worry about improvised explosive devices (IEDs) during convoys, suicide bombers, or any other not-so-fun things. What I did not realize was how many obstacles I would have to face each day at school. The difference is that now most of these conflicts are internal rather than external.

One of the most difficult aspects of being in school is remembering that I am not in the Army anymore. In many ways, the military and college lifestyles clash with each other. Life in the military is structured, and many routines are standardized across duty stations. Therefore, it is a shock to see an ROTC cadet in uniform doing something that would not have been allowed when I was in uniform. As much as I would like to correct them on their action, I really cannot because I am no longer in the service.

Of course, I realize that a college student who is straight out of high school, or has never been in a combat situation, does not have to go through what a combat vet has to go through each day in addition to studying. Going to combat is something that an enlisted person has accepted, but accepting that responsibility does not make it much easier. Regardless of how Hollywood or video game companies portray it, war still sucks. For me, the hardest part is dealing with the memories of the war and attending school simultaneously, because I am dealing with Post-Traumatic Stress Disorder (PTSD). The war I went through didn't end when I came home, and now I feel like a new war has started.

Waking each morning is difficult for me. There were, and still are, times when my sleep is not as restful as I would like it to be. Most students would say they were up late cramming for exams or just plain old studying. To be honest, I really wish I could say that all the time to make myself feel better. There are nights when I wake from my nightmares screaming bloody murder or catch myself fighting someone who is not there. The real scary part is when you almost harm your loved one by accident. It reminds me of the White Bear Theory that I was once taught in my Intro to Psychology class: the more you tell yourself to forget the bear, the more it lingers. At this point, I sometimes think I would prefer the polar bear! Waking up from such a dream makes it difficult to drive to school and function in class.

Apart from having my nightmares about the war, another reason that it is often hard to get myself to school is because I often feel what I call "flat." Most people are used to responding to their surroundings on multiple levels. They see nuances, respond physically, and feel temperature changes in colors. In a nutshell, they have emotions. Sometimes I wake up with no feelings or cares at all. It is not that I am antisocial—I still have Jiminy Cricket on my shoulder. It's just that I feel apathetic. Part of the frustration is that I don't even always know why I feel this way. All I know is that when I feel that way, going to school seems pointless. Of course, these symptoms are characteristic of Post-Traumatic Stress Disorder.

Knowing that you have the disorder doesn't make it easier to cope with it. To make matters worse, thanks to Hollywood, many people assume that people with PTSD are likely to snap at a moment's notice, turn into Rambo, and kill someone. Increasing media coverage of PTSD has certainly led many members of the general public to assume that all former military members are likely to be unpredictable and angry. This may contribute to the feeling I share with other vets that I am an outsider on campus, because I have no idea of how I would be accepted by people when they realize what I am dealing with. Even though I have friends who have accepted me for who I am, the fear lingers each day, and it is hard not to worry about being stigmatized.

While I was in college during my second-to-last semester at the University of Texas at San Antonio (UTSA), I realized that I could not take failure with a grin. Most students, at any stage of education, do not see a failing grade as an end to their education, and that is understandable. Many will want to attend a higher level of schooling, just as I do. Failure, for me, was a different story. It took me a while to realize that a failure does not have the same consequences that would follow if I had failed while in the Army. If I should fail at any moment during my service in the Army, the missions may not be accomplished, but the darker side is that there could be casualties.

This is not to say that I am a perfectionist, because really, if you knew me, I am not that at all. With this idea being ingrained into my training, failing was something that was avoided as much as possible. You do not want to be the one having that burden on you for the rest of your life. Failing at something still does not feel good, but at least I am now able to see it in a different light. Still, many of my veteran friends and I wonder how we can feel so stressed in an environment where our decisions are not life or death.

I am proud to say that as of May 2013, I achieved my first academic goal and graduated from the University of Texas at San Antonio with a Bachelor of Arts degree in psychology. I am currently seeking employment, and hopefully by the time you read this I will be gainfully employed and/or have won the Publisher's Clearing House Sweepstakes or Powerball lottery. In all seriousness, going to war and going to school are not easy for veterans, but it is impossible to calculate the value of spending the time and effort necessary to help veterans use the skills they developed in the military to succeed in school so they can go on to benefit their civilian communities as well.

Thank you for reading my story. I hope it gives you a brief glimpse into what we veterans deal with in these transitions in our lives and careers.

BRANDI CUEVAS
ARMY

Brandi is the student who always sits near the front of the class, listens intently to every word of the lecture, and over prepares for exams. Therefore, it was a surprise to me when I found out that attending college was only a small aspect of her very busy life. As an active member in the Reserve, a parent of two young daughters, and the wife of a soldier who was recently deployed again, she somehow still found time to complete her undergraduate degree, and is now pursuing a master's degree.

I remember sitting in the audience during my junior year of high school, waiting to take a general aptitude test. I was informed that if I volunteered to take it, I could get out of at least three hours of class. Having learned the art of test-taking, I also knew that it wouldn't take me nearly that long to complete it, and I could sneak in some *zzzzz*'s. I had no idea at the time how much that test—the Armed Services Vocational Aptitude Battery (ASVAB)—would change my life.

Peers of mine used to think I was crazy. Why would I spend my childhood racing 150 miles an hour to achieve my goals, instead of chilling with everyone else? I can recall numerous times when I begged my mom to ground me so that I would have a good excuse to tell people that I couldn't go out when they invited me. Quite frankly, I enjoyed my alone moments to contemplate life and tackle the next project at hand.

I was involved in a touring singing group of thirty or so ladies called Cantatrice, along with another larger choir group. I was president of Distributive Education Clubs of America (DECA), Secretary of Cantatrice, and the historian of the mountaineering club. Along with a full load of classes and part-time jobs, I was nominated to be the high school representative for Junior Achievement, which gave me the added responsibility of meeting with business executives from the leading companies in Salt Lake City (Deseret News, Franklyn Covey, etc.) Needless to say, I was exhausted. I spent moments daydreaming of snuggling up on the couch with a good book rather than going to the movies with friends.

Months passed, and I thought nothing of the ASVAB scores that I received. Someone told me that I scored high enough to select any job I wanted, but the Army was never a thought in my mind. Later that summer, however, my world was turned upside down. In the middle of spending my vacation with family, I called my boyfriend to hear his voice and recap the details of my journey. I could tell right away from the conversation that something was wrong. I was disheartened; I had a sinking feeling in my chest, and the perma-grin smile quickly dissipated from my face. No sooner had I come to the realization that I had fallen for him completely and wholeheartedly than he disappeared from my life.

The rest of my summer vacation was no longer filled with fleeting butterflies and leaping on clouds. I was devastated. I fell into a depressed state. When I arrived home, the magnitude of what had really taken place hit me. My boyfriend had run away from home, started dating a whole slew of other girls, and everyone else already knew about it. It was hard to escape high school gossip and the crowd of friends I had become accustomed to hanging out with, especially when we all enjoyed the same activities in a small town. It was even harder to see someone I cared so much about hanging on someone else. In my mind, I could dig a hole no deeper. I was in a bottomless pit of agony. My heart could barely withstand the wrenching pain.

After two months of wallowing in my misery, a thought occurred to me: if I was already at the very, very bottom, then there was nothing I could do to get any lower. Any step I took could only keep me in the same position or propel me forward. I had to do something. I could not let a measly boy conquer me! I could not let him affect my life, my decisions—my path. I had too much at stake and too much potential to let it go to waste.

I made a split decision to engross myself in learning about health and exercise, and I frequented the library. I stuck my nose in the pages of every article I could find, earning the classic nickname, "bookworm." I became the person whose paper everyone glanced at before they circled their final answer on an exam. My brain was a sponge! I had never felt so connected to my inner thoughts. I learned to respond to (in the words of one of my supervisors) my "exquisite self-awareness."

It was at this time that a recruiter ventured into my life. Staff Sergeant Baxter (not her real name) made no guarantees; she only said, "I think you will enjoy this based on what I have heard about your interests so far." SSG Baxter came to my home to discuss my curiosity about the Army with my parents—since I was only seventeen at the time, I needed my parents' permission to proceed with any actions. Reluctantly, Mom and Dad signed the dotted line allowing me to have control over my own decisions when dealing with the military. I later found out that Dad was secretly jumping for joy. He had always threatened to kick me out at the age of eighteen; here I was making his life easier and leaving without a fight. An appointment was scheduled with the Military Entrance Processing Station (MEPS), launching me into what would be the longest-standing career of my life thus far.

Taking a big gulp, I called my mom one afternoon to relay the details of my day. I asked her to sit down. What I had to tell her was very important, and I needed her to understand my thought processes. "Mom, I joined the United States Army Reserve (USAR). I have already sworn my life away, and I leave one week after graduation for basic training." I wasn't prepared for the flood of tears on the other end of the line and the incessant, "Are you sure this is what you want to do?"

Later that night when I finally returned home, my mom rushed me over to the leader of our church. We were members of the Church of Jesus Christ of Latter Day Saints (Mormons), and all my mom could think of was that I had made the worst decision of my life in one rash moment. The bishop took a moment to ask me a few questions and clarify the details of what had transpired. I didn't expect anyone to believe me.

To this day, I have practiced living the motto, "no regrets," so I told him, point blank, that "I felt prompted to join and I couldn't deny my feeling." He then offered me a blessing, one that I have cherished throughout my life when recalling the true reason why I am a soldier today and why I continue to march on. Specifically, he said that I was called to serve, and that this was my mission in life. He told me that people would thank me for introducing them to Jesus Christ and that I would be a beacon for good. I didn't understand then what that really meant. Was I to be a missionary? I hated preaching, and I certainly didn't plan on converting anyone. In fact, I enjoyed the diversity of religion and culture.

Word spread like wildfire through my senior-year high school class. Any time someone mentioned even the thought of joining any branch of the armed services, the recruiters referred them to me. Suddenly I became a *big deal*. I had countless friends, associates, and complete strangers ask me, "Why did you do it?" I was told that when I got asked out, many of the guys were too scared to get too close to me or to even try and steal a kiss because "they thought that I would beat them for trying." I guess I might have, if I had not wanted it. However, I would have done that with or without the "soldier" label.

My ex-boyfriend came back into my life for a short period of time. He was concerned that I had made a bad decision. A flurry of thoughts raced through my mind. Who was he to judge? We weren't even dating anymore. Why would he care? Why would I need his permission? The last thing he had told me before he dumped me was, "Please, never join the Army." It was as if it was destined. He knew somehow that the military would be a positive influence in my life. I had promised that I wouldn't sign on the dotted line, but I guess I lied. I didn't join out of spite; I joined to be true to myself! Six months later, he decided to join as well. I never questioned his motives. Maybe, subconsciously, I knew that he, too, had a mission to accomplish as a soldier.

Graduation came and went. I spent some time saying goodbye to friends, celebrating the close of a chapter in my life and the opening of a new novel of experiences. I had a couple of going-away parties; my favorite was when the football team and soccer teams wished me off and ate my family out of house and home. I loved the great big bear hugs from the linemen and the chiseled quads of the soccer boys.

On the day of my departure to Fort Leonard Wood, Missouri (Fort Lost-in-the-Woods, for those who have been before), I packed the bare necessities: a couple of sets of civilian clothes, pajamas, personal hygiene items, scriptures, and some *pogey* bait (snacks and treats). I cannot describe the emotions I felt and how quickly they bounced from fear to excitement, dread to exhilaration. Would I miss my family? Would I make it through the horror stories of drill sergeants? Would I break down and cry showing my weakness—that I was just a girl? What would my friends back home be doing? Who would be dating whom? Who would go to college in the fall? Did I really make the right decision?

The first couple of days, groups of people arrived at different times. We were herded into long lines to "hurry up and wait." In-processing took a lot of time. We had only two days to get all our affairs in order. This included filling out paperwork for emergency contacts, life insurance, direct deposits, and so forth. We were all issued a standard amount of money to be able to purchase what we needed from the assigned packing list and given time to shop.

This was the life! I couldn't figure out why so many people complained about basic training. I was fed three square meals a day. I could choose from a variety of different main courses, fruits, vegetables, and desserts. I had my own bed and locker. There was no one yelling at me or forcing me to do anything. Occasionally a new recruit would arrive and be harassed for his long, bright red locks, but after a speedy trip to the barber, there were no more issues.

Then came the day of reckoning: the day we met our drill sergeants. As we stood, packed like sardines with deer-in-the-headlights looks on our faces, we could hear the rumble of a mass of motorcycles. I used to love listening to the sound of Harleys, but on that particular morning, I was scared to death. One bike after another pulled up in the parking lot of the building we were crowded into. I could hear the kickstands whip out and dig into the gravel. Crunch. Stomp. Stomp. As I waited for each one to park, I lost count of how many had arrived. Then there was silence. It seemed like an eternity.

"Which one of you maggots is going to be graced with my presence?" roared one of the riders as he brushed through the doorway. "I want that one." "No, he's mine. You take the other one. He doesn't look like he'd last a minute." One by one, each of us was turned around and examined. I remember thinking that if this was just some mind trick, it was working: they sure scared the hell out of me.

I was nearly the last one to make the cut. My self-esteem was sinking quickly. Was I not up to par? What were they whispering about while they eyed me? I pictured the drill sergeants playing rock–paper–scissors. The one who begrudgingly called me out, "Private Taylor," must have lost the match.

In my best drill and ceremony (rehearsed while watching a recruiting commercial), I left-faced, marched right out the door, and herded, literally, onto a cattle truck. Images of trucks crammed full of cows, with flies buzzing all around, on their way to the slaughterhouse, flashed through my mind. Was basic training really as bad as the embellished stories passed along the rumor mill? It was the middle of June and smoldering hot. Having all this fresh meat squished together certainly didn't help my morale. I tried to dissociate from the situation and picture myself at home, stress free. Once the truck stopped, however, I was immediately reminded of the reality of the situation.

"You have ten seconds to get everyone off this truck or you will all be pushing until the sun goes down. One … Two … Three …" This was no joke. They were serious. And I was about to be seriously smoked (forced to work out until my limbs became Jell-o). We turned into a crazy mob, pushing each other trying to grab all of our belongings. Some of us rushed down the plank. Others spilled over the sides, grasping to latch on to something and be saved from the fall. There were drill sergeants all over, yelling. I had one follow me, two inches from my face, spitting as he told me to "Hurry your @ss up. Faster! Faster!" Grown men were crying, trying unsuccessfully to fight the tears.

Groundhog Day became the norm. Each morning, we were awakened to the sound of metal spoons beating on metal trash cans—Bang! Bang! Bang!—followed by processions of screaming and yelling, "Good moooornnninnggg, ladies. You've been asleep waaaay too long. I have had my beauty sleep. It's time for you to get up now. You have three seconds. One ... Two ..." After what felt like a minor heart attack, I rolled out of bed trying to smooth down my hair, which had doubled in size due to the humidity. Unsteady on feet covered by white calf-high socks, I wiped the boogies from my eyes and skidded out to the hallway. Black bags hung underneath my swollen lids and I spewed dragon breath while I belted out the official song of the United States Army: "First to fight for the right, and to build the nation's might, and the Army goes rolling along ..."

The rule at basic training, according to some manual or regulation, was that every soldier needed at least eight hours of rest per day. What they didn't specify is how the eight hours were allotted. I learned very quickly that my nights would not be safe from the grueling demands of the enforcers. Some nights we were whistled out of bed to exercise. Other nights we were awakened with a flashlight in our faces, telling us it was time for our charge of quarters (CQ) duty. And then on rare occasions, we were left alone for a night. It was during those times that I would sneak away to the latrine (the only place in the building where a drill sergeant wouldn't come in to harass me) and write letters home.

As the weeks progressed, I began the transformation from civilian to soldier. I began rehearsing the Army General Orders while donning a protective mask and wearing it around the room at night. I figured that if I could get used to walking around and breathing in it, I could erase my fear of suffocation.

One night when I was in this mode, I started rehearsing the nonverbal signs for a gas attack warning. While I was walking around curling my biceps with fists clenched tight, a roommate of mine started screaming. She, too, had been experiencing nightmares of being caught off guard; seeing me only confirmed that she had slept through an attack. She jumped out of bed and started grabbing her gear, screaming, "Gas, gas, gas!!!" It took some time to convince her that I was only practicing before she crawled back into bed and fell asleep.

Another roommate of mine was assigned as my battle buddy, merely because I stood up for her when the drill sergeants started picking on her. We were nicknamed "peas in a pod" because we claimed to have the same birthplace. In actuality, I was somewhat mortified to be her sidekick. I could look past her inability to complete one pushup or one sit-up—that was something that, with practice, she could overcome. But what I had trouble understanding was the fact that she would rarely shower. She rolled up her nasty, smelly undergarments and placed them back in her locker without laundering. She would sit atop the bunk bed in our room picking scabs and eating them for periods of time. Images of her squatting in formation, farting and giggling, haunt me to this day. She reminded me of an unclassy Yogi Bear covered in fuzz, with hair sticking out every which way. Later on, during training, she ended up firing her weapon down range during a cease-fire—endangering the Command Sergeant Major who was giving a speech in that direction—and was immediately processed out of the military.

Our schedules were packed with drill sergeant-led classes about the Army's stance on families, leadership, values, and soldiering. Interspersed throughout the day were periods of "smoke sessions" (flutter kicks, pushups, sit-ups, sprints, etc.) and soldiering skills (high-low crawl, drill and ceremony, weapons handling, etc.). At one point during training, I surpassed a drill sergeant in a competition of crunches, earning the right to perform pushups each time any drill sergeant called out my name—twenty in each cardinal direction: north, south, east, and west.

Every time one class ended, another one started. Every new class meant a new instructor. You can imagine how many pushups I completed throughout the course of a sixteen-hour day. I even pushed for each letter of mail that I received. Being a good pen pal, I never fell short of at least fifty pushups at mail call. I hurt in places I never even knew possible.

The grueling monotony of sleep deprivation, physical exhaustion, and incessant name calling chiseled away part of my "individual-ness." The constant demand to create the "perfect soldier" made it hard for anyone to have a sense of uniqueness. We were an assembly line of parts being molded by the situation we found ourselves in.

By nature, I dance to my own drum, so I learned to strategically maintain a positive outlook on the situation by making the mundane interesting. I contemplated how I could make people laugh and how I could make the most uncomfortable situations easier to handle. One day, as I walked into the latrine lined with rows of toilets on each side (with no doors), I embraced my quirkiness. Saddling up to the seat—only two feet away from the next—and facing my comrades to the left, right, and front flanks, I stretched out my arms: "Incoming!!! Gas, gas, gas!!!" The shocked faces were priceless. I could only imagine their thoughts: "What was she doing?" I looked at them and let it rip, enjoying the moment of freedom to perform normal bodily functions without the restraint of worrying about whether someone could hear or smell my plop. Success never tasted so sweet.

The females were treated vastly differently from the males. My cohort of comrades was the first class to have integrated male and female barracks (males inhabiting the top floors, with females located on the lower levels) and training. Many of the male drill sergeants had no clue how to treat females in the military, struggling with the conflict between the societal norm of being chivalrous towards women and the need for discipline in the Army.

One drill sergeant met with me face to face. I cannot remember what I did, but I do recall the thought that I had done something very stupid, to the point that even my dad would have chastised me. This drill sergeant however, pursed his lips, refraining from reflexive ridicule. I could see the red rise from his neck like mercury in a thermometer. As it rose towards his wrinkled forehead, my eyes widened. For a moment, I feared for what would take place. Then he released his venom, "Flowers!!!!" and stormed off. I looked around, unable to speak. We were all shocked. Did he really say that? When I finally gathered my wits, I mused about what had just happened. "Wow!" I thought to myself. "The adopted no-swearing policy really is in effect." Would he have had the same reaction if I was a man?

One day, with one hand tucked inside a dirt-ridden boot and the other making small circles with a kiwi-caked towel, I had spit-shined for what seemed like hours when a soldier in my squad walked toward me. She looked troubled. It wasn't very often that we had the opportunity to contact our loved ones, friends, or family to discuss personal matters. Instead, we learned to rely on those around us. Private Second Class (PV2) "Smith" (not her real name) asked if she could speak to me, and I happily obliged. I loved engaging in meaningful conversation, and welcomed the opportunity to make a new friend.

She proceeded to tell me that she had been dreaming about a fellow soldier and didn't know what to do. She said that she had fallen for this person—could remember the way this person smelled and what this person was wearing when they met. PV2 "Smith" was aware of the rules; we all were—they were crammed down our throats on a daily basis. Fraternization was forbidden and strictly enforced. There were cases of soldiers getting caught and facing punishment (out-processing from the military, additional duties, etc.) depending on the severity of the situation.

I continued to listen to her plight, wondering where this conversation was leading. Then it hit me: she was talking about me! Fraternization was known as an infraction during basic training, but homosexuality was an outright sin. "Don't Ask, Don't Tell" was in effect, and, as a leader, I was obligated to report this violation.

But I had spent the last month getting to know her. She was finally accomplishing a major goal she had longed to achieve since elementary school. As the breadwinner of her family, she was providing a life for her mom and siblings that they had never experienced. Yet I felt I had the power to rip her success out from under her feet. I fretted over what to do. I could not ostracize her. I too cared about her. She had become one of my good friends and confidants. After taking a moment to process all of this information, I calmly asked her to leave so I could figure out what to do. I felt as if I had been hit by a bag of rocks. My heart was heavy. My mind was full, and adrenaline raced through my body. What do I do with this information?

I started to panic somewhat. I had this person who envisioned me as a lover watching me as I undressed, taking showers with me, sharing intimate experiences with me. I could choose to ignore the fact that she, too, is a person who has aspirations, and make a formal complaint. Or I could choose to honor the fact that she felt comfortable enough to share her innermost secrets with me.

Gathering my guts, I met with PV2 "Smith" the next day. I told her that I did not feel the same about her, but that I respected her for being open and honest with me. I set some boundaries and asked her to refrain from sharing those kinds of details with me. I reminded her of our military obligations. In return, she respected my wishes, and ended up becoming a cherished friend!

Halfway through basic training, one of the guys in my platoon had an emotional breakdown. This recent high-school graduate had received an acceptance letter into college granting him a full-ride scholarship to play basketball. He wasn't someone who was out of shape, or someone who just couldn't handle the daily demands of basic training; he was someone looking for the best outcome for his future. I remember seeing him break down, physically sobbing. As the tears rolled down his face, he was escorted to the commander to discuss the situation. The next day, he was loaded onto a plane back home to begin a new pathway into academia.

It was at this time that I had a fleeting moment of consideration to obtain a higher education. No one in my family had ever graduated from college. Apparently, my dad had attended a vocational school for a short period of time, but had eventually given up on that idea. The whole time I was growing up, I never really knew if he had even graduated high school.

I never knew of my mom's intent with regards to school either. In our family dynamic, Mom and Dad both had to work to provide for three kids and a dog. Mom sometimes refrained from working to spend a little more quality time with us, but it was never for an extended period of time. The only mention of a secondary education came from one of my teachers in high school, after I took a first-place trophy home from a state DECA competition. My project focused on Junior Achievement and the effects of mentorship on young children. The teacher felt that I had a lot more potential than to throw my life away in the Army.

I could have applied for scholarships, but my heart was set on a path which I was drawn to. I felt that the Army was my lifelong calling, and I was determined to apply for active duty once I finished my training.

The cessation of basic training resulted in family visitations and a graduation ceremony. Before sending an invitation back home, I was bombarded with vivid dreams of finally being able to slide a pair of jeans on. I missed being feminine and all that entailed (makeup, blow dryers, curling irons, perfume, etc.). I had nightmares that, during the course of soldiering, I had forgotten how to be a girl. Why did this bother me so much? I hated being just a number.

According to the federal government, that is exactly what I was—Social Security number *721-**-****.* I embraced all facets of my kaleidoscopic self. In the course of ten weeks, I had grown from being a fledgling to learning how to soar on my own.

Wearing my spiffed-up Class A uniform and shiny shoes, I stared out at the audience looking for a familiar face. I didn't recognize a single soul. Rows upon rows of smiling faces greeted their soldiers. I yearned to see my mom, to hug her and hold her close. To tell her I was sorry for all the times I was a brat. Suddenly, an announcement screeched through the microphone, and a drill sergeant, who appeared to be glaring at me with a smug grin of victory, said, "Some flights have been delayed. The passengers will be waiting at the barracks once they arrive."

I was devastated. I longed to have a congratulatory party sharing the joy of what I had accomplished. I knew my mom would be a teary mess. The culmination of adolescence evolving into adulthood was a once-in-a-lifetime opportunity, and, against her own will, she would miss it.

The drill sergeants took full advantage of the opportunity and assigned a couple of us the additional duty of tearing down the decorations, folding up the chairs, and loading the bus. As the bus pulled up to the barracks an hour after everyone else had dispersed, I saw Mom, red-faced with bloodshot eyes, waiting at the corner of the street. How long had she been waiting? We made eye contact. She began to rush towards me, but the bus did not stop. It continued forward, with my mom following quickly behind. As it pulled to a stop, the drill sergeants ordered me to unload the bus before I could spend time with my loved one. I seethed. I should have disobeyed and hugged my mom. Instead, I looked at her, mouthing, "Just a moment," pleading with her to be understanding and patient. With the last chair resting in the closet, I finally embraced my mom. I breathed a sigh of relief, and a flood of pent-up emotions engulfed her. I cried. My shoulders fell. My body went limp as she held me. I had needed to be strong for so long.

With the flight delay, I had only thirteen hours to spend with my mom before I had to report back to duty. We checked into a hotel room off base. Mom relayed the details of her flight: there was some equipment malfunction; the passengers were all held up on the runway for hours; they had to deplane and wait for another flight crew to arrive. I patiently listened to what she had to say, about ready to burst. Then she handed me wrapped gifts and said, "I believe this is what you wanted." I gently tore off the lid and peered in. The first box was a collection of homemade goodies. Mom's best friend spoiled me. I took a bite of the three-inch Oreo cookie made from scratch.

The next package will forever remain seared in my mind. Upon opening the package, I quickly undressed, grabbing for my Luckys. One by one, I slid my newly shaved legs into the cool, smooth jeans. A smirk quickly grew on my lips. I looked at my mom and dashed toward the other queen-sized bed.

Throwing out all sense of reason, and with complete disregard for Grandma's constant scolding, I started jumping. I jumped higher and higher. Mom started giggling. This was heaven on earth. In a flash, I tore out the black bands holding together the bun in my hair, letting it fall to my shoulders. I headed to the mirror and started blow-drying with a curl brush, defying the image that I was no longer feminine. I slid on a necklace and put on a pair of earrings. I powdered my nose. And that's how I remained the rest of that night—all dolled up.

The morning after was bittersweet. I had to again say goodbye to my mom once again. I promised to return home during the holidays, but that was still months away. Accountability was taken, and each of us was assigned to a different charter bus traveling to the next duty assignment. I was relieved to find that I wasn't the only one from my company to head towards Fort Sam Houston for advanced individual training (AIT). It was common knowledge that we would have more freedom during AIT. What a relief! I looked forward to some normalcy. As the bus came to a halt, I awoke with drool sliding down my face; I must have fallen asleep during the ride. Seconds later, a drill sergeant charged onto the bus and started barking orders. I thought basic training was over—what happened?

We were quickly shuttled off the bus. The person next to me tripped as she stepped down from the ledge. A military photographer took a picture (which eventually plastered the front page of Fort Sam Houston's News Leader) of her stumble as she met face-to-face with Drill Sergeant Jennings, who began sputtering invented and downgraded expletives.

She was ordered to start pushing for being so clumsy. Since I was in the near vicinity, I was automatically assigned as her battle buddy and had to start pushing alongside her. The conflicting images of what I thought AIT was going to be like and what it truly was made it hard to maintain motivation. What was the real meaning to all of this? What was I supposed to learn? My high school friends were heading off to college, getting married, and having babies. What was the purpose of the path I was on? I felt like I was in survival mode.

Fast forward six months. Returning to the civilian world as an Army Reservist was a major adjustment. Soldiers use different lingo than civilians—acronyms like LDRSHIP, which stands for the Army values; jargon like hoo-ah (acknowledging agreement with whoever is speaking) and ate-up (someone who doesn't meet expected outcomes); or common courtesies (saluting, responding with "Yes, ma'am," standing at attention for the raising of the flag). There was no command giving me directions as to when to get out of bed or when to eat. I did not have a preplanned schedule of goals to achieve. I could sleep in my own bed, use my own shower, and eat at will. I didn't have to ask for permission to go out dancing. There was no curfew. There was no signing out when I left my area. There was no collectivist culture. Teamwork was almost frowned upon, while independence and self-sufficiency were heralded.

To make matters worse, my father had become a drunkard while I was gone. On numerous occasions, my family arrived home from work or school to find the front door wide open and my dad passed out beneath the doorframe. Mom served Dad with divorce papers. She no longer wanted the poor quality of life that Dad attracted with his drinking. My siblings were still minors going to school. Mom had to keep them safe and provide for their needs.

Living on my own for the past year left me feeling trapped at home, fighting the urge to take charge of the situation, and wanting to knock some sense into my dad with a two-by-four. I decided to move out of state and start anew. Dad's parting words, in a drunken stupor, were, "I am envious of you and what you are making of your life. I only wish I would have done the same." His words were a catalyst that helped me press forward with a determination to deflect anything in my path to success.

I used my government-issued (GI) benefits to apply for automatic in-state residency and began the process of applying for school. Where I lived at the time, there were no military installations nearby with education centers I could visit. However, each university and college had a Department of Veterans Affairs (VA) office. The personnel in that office, either veterans themselves or "military brats" raised by parents in the armed services, were all too eager to help a new veteran student process into university life.

My initial contract with the military granted me a $7,521.48 Montgomery GI Bill (MGIB) payment in return for six years of satisfactory participation in the USAR and two years of inactive ready reserve (IRR). USAR requirements equated to two to three days' attendance at monthly battle assemblies (BA) and two to three weeks of annual training (AT) per year, while IRR was used as a holding tank for the federal government to quickly "beef up" personnel during times of crisis. Soldiers in the IRR did not have to attend BAs or ATs; they only had to remain available if called up to serve.

The paperwork was daunting: I needed a signed Notice of Basic Eligibility (NOBE) proving my entitlement to the MGIB; my Leave and Earning Statement (LES) had to state that I was a current resident of that state; and I had to show proof of legal residency, using documents like copies of utility bills. The decision to grant me in-state residency took a few weeks.

In the meantime, I registered for classes, submitting the transmittal to the VA for processing. I registered with GoArmyEd to receive tuition assistance (TA), a separate benefit for those actively drilling with their units. MGIB plus TA amounted to 100 percent coverage for tuition and books, along with a couple of hundred dollars extra per month for ancillary costs.

I took great pride in the fact that I was a soldier. Here I was just barely out of high school, yet I was years ahead of many of the people around me, with hands-on, working knowledge of the "real world" outside of Mom and Dad's grasp. The military taught me how to work efficiently with little to no supervision or guidance.

I knew I had to be involved in various university organizations as a means to network and figure out the hidden tricks of the trade as a student, so I hosted a physical fitness activity (military style) during one of the meetings of a collegiate fraternity. Enacting my best drill sergeant impression—"Hup, two, three, four. Pick it up, two, three, four,"—I made my fellow students sweat bullets, running around the parking lot and performing calisthenics round-robin style. Most of them could not keep up and were amazed at my stamina. I was asked to speak at conferences to relay my thoughts on the military, leadership, and the ability to exercise my spirituality. Several people stopped to ask me about my military experience and what I would recommend for their own lives. I felt like I had become some so-called military prodigy.

Employment was somewhat easy to come by. Most employers were excited to hear about my expertise with the military, and I had several interviews lined up. However, my options were limited. Of the two military occupations—field medic and surgical technologist—I had certified for, only the field medic position qualified for licensure. I certified on the National Registry of Emergency Medical Technicians Basic (NREMT-B) exam. The surgical technologist position had given me hundreds of hours of on-the-job training, but the subject matter did not meet the standards for an approved civilian program. It was difficult to find a job that utilized my skill set; most hospitals that were hiring required years of experience, along with professional credentials.

To make matters worse, where I lived there was an imbalance between Allied Health employees' salaries versus banking and call center positions. As an EMT and first responder, I would have made slightly above minimum wage; while working as a customer service representative I would make 50 percent more. Rather than volunteer at an organization in order to increase my odds of getting hired, I needed to find employment that would cover housing, medical and dental insurance, and groceries. I found that sitting at a desk was far from optimal, however, and kept getting antsy for a little more excitement. I debated about whether I should join the active duty Army, switch branches, or apply for a Reserve Officer Training Corps (ROTC) scholarship and go to school full-time. I completed an application for active duty, but something unconsciously kept me from submitting the forms.

I advanced through the ranks fairly quickly; within my first six months of the delayed entry program (DEP), I moved from Private (PVT) to Private 2 (PV2), on account of recruiting more than three people. I moved from PV2 to Private First Class (PFC) following AIT graduation, earning Specialist rank within the next year. I made sergeant (SGT) by my fifth year of service. I volunteered for additional missions and signed up for leadership courses. Over the course of two years, I traveled on official government business for the military to Washington, Oklahoma, Texas, New Jersey, Wisconsin, and Colorado.

During the time I was working on my Associate of Arts (AA) degree in general studies, the tragic events of September 11th kept me and my soon-to-be-husband on alert, moving our proposed wedding date up two months. We knew we were better protected as a couple if we were married (next of kin [NOK] updates, medical/dental/life insurance, etc.), especially with the uproar of terrorism and the threat of mobilization and/or deployment. With only two months to plan our wedding, I rescinded my acceptance to start training for the police academy, cancelled my enrolled in school, moved to another state, and requested a transfer to my husband's military unit.

Managing civilian employment, military duty, and higher education seemed like a fairly easy venture until I got married to another service member (my high school sweetheart) who had to juggle the same kinds of demands. We had a mutual understanding that he would be the breadwinner when we decided to start a family, thus making it mandatory for him to have a stellar work experience. By contrast, my resume became a scattered mess of civilian jobs and undergraduate programs. The only thing that remained constant was the fact that I was a member of the US Army Reserve.

The whole idea of not having roots seemed to be commonplace for us. In fact, my husband and I couldn't stay in one place for too long. We would get what we termed "the itch," and scout out possibilities for new adventures. Maybe that is one of the reasons we have lasted so long in the military—we enjoy the lifestyle of always being on the move.

As a couple, we volunteered for many different opportunities. We were able to work with Homeland Defense during a collapsed structure training exercise that mimicked the events of 9/11. We attended a mass casualty decontamination exercise integrating civilian first responders with military personnel. We traveled to Germany to work in the hospitals caring for soldiers arriving from down range (the war zone).

I was constantly trying to figure out what I really wanted to do in my life. The military helped me by providing paid training and educational benefits, but I often wondered how I could tie both of those worlds together. There was only a handful of military occupation specialties (MOSs) that afforded the opportunity to take the national certification exam for licensure. I had already experienced the difficulty of trying to find a job that both matched what I was getting paid on active duty training status and implemented my previous military training.

I requested an additional MOS as a radiologic technologist and was accepted for training. It was during that training that I received orders sending me to Iraq. When I called to ask for the details of the deployment, I was told that they were looking for a medic with a certain rank. I informed them that I was being reclassed into a different occupation, and the orders were rescinded.

Since I was at the top of my class during training, I was able to select the location for my internship. I selected Walter Reed in Washington, DC, and, to my surprise, I got it! Little did I know how much this location would affect me. Soldiers with severe and debilitating injuries from down range were prepped for flight and evacuated to Walter Reed for further treatment and care. I saw soldiers who had fought for the land of the free struggling to survive. Tears came to my eyes as one of my patients picked me up, spun me around, and proceeded to dance with me, saying, "I can dance better with these legs than I ever could with my real ones." That phrase will forever remain seared in my memory.

At the conclusion of my internship, my husband and I decided that it was time to expand our family. Pregnancy was definitely not an easy endeavor for me! I vomited throughout the duration, and even on my way to the delivery room. For a majority of the pregnancy, I was mobilized, and I traveled for Homeland Defense twice a month, giving classes on medical parameters within a chemical, biological, radiological, nuclear, and high-yield explosive (CBRNE) environment.

I had to suit up in my husband's uniform in order to meet clothing standards for being on duty. I lived out of suitcases in hotel rooms the entire duration, some nights wrapping my arms around my belly, sobbing silently. I wanted to have my baby, but the lifestyle I lived seemed to be at odds with the conventional, socially constructed lifestyle of a mom. I grew up thinking I was supposed to stay at home, "barefoot, pregnant, and in the kitchen," as my dad would always put it. But that statement rubbed me wrong in all sorts of ways. I had challenged the image my parents and church had conceptualized for me by leaving for the Army. Now I was challenging the idea of being a soldier and a mother at the same time. How could I respond to Uncle Sam's call, yet put my family first?

On my baby's first birthday, September 11th, I was called in to the hospital for a stat case. I had to leave my daughter's party and all the guests to respond to the emergency. I remember how my heart ached for leaving her, how I would miss the memories of her opening her gifts.

It was then that the epiphany hit—I would use my GI benefits and go back to school. That would ensure that I was still out of the house part-time, which would keep me from going stir-crazy. I would receive stipends that amounted to a part-time job, increase my opportunities for promotion or commissioning, and be debt free.

Jobless and pregnant with my second baby, I applied to the University of Texas at San Antonio (UTSA) and was accepted into their Bachelor of Arts in Psychology program. I had to submit transcripts from all sources of higher education, past history of employment, and references. My resume included a history of attending four different colleges and universities to complete my Associate of Arts degree in general education. It had taken only eight years, across three states, to complete.

The credit hours applied from previous military training ended up equaling more than one hundred elective credit hours, and other school credits were also added to my degree plan. I embraced my VA benefits; as a current reservist I qualified for 75 percent tuition reimbursement, and my GI Bill benefits equaled a couple of hundred dollars per month.

Upon earning my BA degree in psychology, I was hesitant to apply for graduation and lose all of the credit hours I had earned serving in the military. Instead, I signed up for a dual degree and started earning credits towards a Bachelor of Science degree in kinesiology. Attending fitness and nutrition classes daily sparked an interest in incorporating both degree plans—sport and exercise psychology.

Using that frame of reference, I became involved in various programs that would help me bring my goal to fruition. I joined the Health Ambassadors (HA)—an organization dedicated to the promotion of health and wellness via community outreach. This included attending diabetes expos, cancer prevention seminars, and performing health assessments: blood pressure reading, glucose/cholesterol screening, muscle-to-fat ratios, etc. I interned at an institute dedicated to the prevention of cancer and the promotion of health and wellness to ensure a better quality of life. My tenure there assisted me in being granted my first authorship, which in turn created opportunities to become a reviewer, present at poster sessions, and be acknowledged at international conferences.

Staff at UTSA invited me to participate in various research opportunities as well. I worked as a student researcher, helping to develop a collection of questionnaires to see how best UTSA could serve the military. I met with the Student Veterans Affairs Organization to discuss pertinent issues facing vets returning to school after being in the fight for so long. At one point I was given the opportunity to read aloud the names of fallen soldiers in commemoration of their service to our country. It was one of the most somber, yet exhilarating, events of my life. Their names will forever be remembered for their ultimate sacrifice, and I played a role in honoring those who had gone before me.

The magnitude of what UTSA was doing for their vets didn't hit me until my husband was handpicked for deployment to Afghanistan. With two toddlers in tow, a full schedule, and internships, I was struggling. My closest family members were five hours away. It helped that both of my kids' birthdays were on holidays (Patriot Day and Independence Day); I never had to ask for time off on those days. But for other times when I needed assistance, I had to call on friends and associates to help me maintain my household.

Fellow classmates at UTSA would occasionally watch my babies on campus while I attended classes. My girls knew how to traverse the campus better than many of the students, and would find the places where it was okay to run, jump, and play. Their favorite areas included the Sombrilla Plaza fountain (water is always a toddler's favorite pastime) and the area between the Howard E. Butt (HEB) Grocery Company University Center and the Convocation Center—grass for miles (at least according to sixteen-inch legs), stray cats, and occasional band performances with free food. Thank God for UTSA's accommodations! Chick-Fil-A was also heaven sent!

My little girls became the mascots of several HA events—future UTSA alumni. My professors never complained, even when they had to face off with a three-year-old rampaging through the bleachers of the classroom, or when the entire class had to listen to me constantly "shoosh" my kids while they giggled at a movie playing in the back of the classroom.

There were moments when I was ready to throw in the towel. I would sit in the corner of my house and cry. Why did going to school, managing children, and being a soldier have to be so hard? There were endless nights of little to no sleep, filled with coughing, runny noses, and fevers. I had to study in the wee hours of the night when the girls slept.

At one point, I was forced to contact a professor and let him know I couldn't make it to the midterm. Knowing my predicament—husband on deployment, no local family, struggling to survive—he allowed me to extend the due date and bring one of my babies in with me to take the exam while she slept. Other professors allowed me to skip class and make up missed assignments by other means—like sending a family photo from Halloween in place of a journal entry. I couldn't believe how catering the professors were to a striving mom.

It only took me thirteen years, three mobilization tours for myself, one deployment for my husband, two dogs (fuzzy kids), and two more kids, but I finally graduated! My diploma read "Summa Cum Laude," with a BS in Kinesiology and a BA in Psychology. I could not have done this without the support from my husband overseas, UTSA faculty, family and friends, and four little chocolate-covered hands grabbing my face and saying, "I love you, mommy."

4

VETERANS GIVING BACK: ALUMNI AND VETERANS AS MENTORS

OTIS SCOTT
AIR FORCE

Otis "Scotty" Scott is a twenty-four-year military veteran who works with UTSA Students and is the Advisor for the UTSA Veteran Students Association. Under his tutelage, the group has focused on getting community organizations involved in helping to find ways to provide a network of support for student Veterans.

THE JOY OF LEARNING

Nelson Mandela once said, "Education is the most powerful weapon which you can use to change the world." If each generation is to do better than the next, its members must be willing to make the sacrifices needed to create the change that they seek. Education is the door to that change, and learning is the key that opens that door. How true that is when we think of the American dream.

If I had known then what I know now, would I have ventured down the path to serve my country, or taken a different path? I would have taken the same path. I realize that even more now as I look back over the years. My education would come during this journey of service.

This story begins long before the early seventies, when I enlisted in the United States Air Force. One might say that I had a passion for travel and service; having been brought up in a military family, I was generally referred to as a "military brat." Having an Army career service member as a father, along with uncles who were also service members (in the Air Force and Navy), might have influenced me in some way, but I was more impressed with the pride, opportunities, and sense of adventure that comes with serving your country.

I grew up in the southern, western, and eastern parts of the United States, specifically Georgia, Alabama, California, and Maryland. I attended more schools than there were grades due to our constant moving—a total of sixteen times, to be exact. Those who have never experienced the constant upheaval of moving and attending many different schools might think that it's terrible having to adjust to new schools, meet new people, and make new friends, all while leaving old friends and classmates behind. To the contrary: it helped in shaping my character and was an education in itself about the many different cultures that make up this diverse and wonderful country in which we live.

Let's just call this a cultural awakening, where your experiences span everything from a more laid-back, culturally pre-civil rights environment to a much more open-minded, culturally aware, free-thinking societal attitude in shaping the culture of our nation—a very diverse culture in and of itself. The things I saw, heard, and experienced all helped me develop in a way that no formal education would have been able to prepare me for.

The culture of the South at that time (the 1950s) was very discriminatory: black citizens were denied their constitutional rights, sharecropping chained African Americans to the land, and their basic liberties were denied. Southern blacks were forced to use separate doctor waiting rooms, drink from water fountains designated for "coloreds," use separate bathrooms, and attend segregated schools that were poor in structure yet rich in educational opportunity. Yes, I lived through all of that.

All of these things, as well as listening to Dr. Martin Luther King on the radio preaching about nonviolent protest while blacks were being relegated to the back of the bus, were all educational experiences in and of them themselves. In the West, people and cultures were mixing and learning from each other. A more revolutionary mindset with a more free-spirited approach to life was unfolding, which often raised questions in my mind about why people were different in the South.

The riots in Los Angeles and Baltimore were all part of an awakening in an attempt to understand why people who fought for change, like President Kennedy and Dr. King, were being assassinated. Why were people of color being lynched, beaten, and bombed? Why were a disproportionate number of African Americans being sent to fight the Vietnamese? Why were people having sit-ins? I saw a change coming, but to understand it, I needed to be educated about what had preceded it and what might be the outcome, based on where we, the American people, were headed.

Even through all of this, there were those who had a profound impact on my thirst for knowledge. Teachers (or educators, as we would refer to them today), my parents, and relatives all helped encourage me and provide the drive: not obtaining an education was not an option. I can clearly hear my mother saying, "Once you get it upstairs, no one can take it away from you," meaning that once you have an education and the knowledge that comes with it, no one can take it from you.

My father established a strong work ethic in my brother and myself. He provided the model and showed us that we needed to work for anything that we obtained. We were not wealthy, but we lived a very comfortable life and never wanted for anything. It goes back to that old adage that says you don't know what you don't have if you have never experienced it. My brother and I were provided a modest allowance until we were teenagers; then one day my father went out and bought a new lawn mower. We thought nothing of it until he pointed to the lawn mower and said, "There is your allowance." That was our first lesson in business and financial management.

My brother and I had plenty of educators surrounding us. My grandmother on my mother's side of the family was an elementary school teacher in the very state where I was born, Georgia. My grandmother on my father's side was a substitute teacher, and my uncle's wife was an elementary school teacher. Unbeknownst to me at the time, this signified the importance of education and the difference that it can make in your life.

Others were also impactful on my journey to higher education. The first that I recall was my sixth grade Spanish teacher. I wished that I had paid more attention, especially in this culturally diverse world that we now live in today, but I get by. The next was my high school English and French teacher, who not only provided me with insight on worldly matters and a much deeper appreciation for music, but also gave me insight into the real estate market. Here again, I wish I had paid a little more attention.

The most impactful was my high school history teacher. Now I have a love for history, not just because of the aspect of learning about the past, but also the lessons that we could learn from the mistakes and achievements made by those in the past, as well as helping to determine the future course of action based on our past mistakes and actions. This history teacher would always inquire about how I was furthering my education whenever I was home visiting my parents. She was never pushy, but she always provided that gentle nudge to keep me going and seeking the knowledge that she knew I would need to make it in the future.

Bouncing, or should I say moving from coast to coast, provided some challenging opportunities as well as some not-so-challenging ones. For instance, elementary school was not very challenging in the South, but was much more so in the western part of the United States. I knew that if I graduated from high school in California, I could go on to attend college at no real cost at that time. This was not meant to be.

We relocated to Maryland when I was in the sixth grade, and I found the curriculum to be just as challenging, but there were more resources for obtaining a well-rounded education in a middle school. Things such as a circular library with an abundance of books, a planetarium to gaze at the stars, controlled environmental animal cages for research and experiments, drafting rooms for architectural design, and wood and metal working shops made a big difference. All in all, this was one of the best schools that I had attended thus far, even after moving three times in the sixth grade. This was the middle school to really challenge me in my educational pursuits.

During that time period, I learned many lessons, both in and out of class, even with some of the distractions that I had. I really wish that I had paid more attention in math class, but when your school was next to an Army research facility, it was kind of difficult to concentrate; flame throwers were going off adjacent to the school, and we saw all sorts of other things going on in the pursuit of advancing military superiority. Living there also provided an education in survival skills that were to prove beneficial later in life. But that's another story.

Let me regress for just a moment. I took an interest in music in the sixth grade; I continued that pursuit in high school, having skipped it in middle school. We moved to Alabama during my high school years, and attending high school there was not as challenging as some of the previous schools I had attended in other states, so naturally I did well, making the National Honor Roll and becoming Editor in Chief of the yearbook.

Another thing that I noticed was that, even in the early '70s, there were no whites or Asians attending the high school, like there would have been in Maryland or California. As a matter of fact, there was a private school built just for the purpose of retaining the segregation between whites and African Americans. Almost twenty years after the US Supreme Court ruled, in

Brown v. Board of Education, that segregated schools were unconstitutional, I was seeing that people were finding ways around the decision.

The one thing that I did learn, more so than anything else, was that I had a voice and speaking up would enable me to have my voice heard. This was the result of a 4-H program that provided a platform for speakers to challenge each other, competing to see who could give the best and most compelling speech. I went on to represent my county at the regional contest, where I spoke on binary numbers and the impact that they would have on our society in the future, especially in developing computers and other technology. If only I had explored that path more aggressively!

The thing that I think I was lacking was a mentor or coach to provide me with a path to higher education. Fortunately, I had a band director who helped a lot. He saw the talent that I had, made me Section Leader, and provided the guidance I needed to obtain a band scholarship to a historically black university (HBU).

Since I graduated with an opportunity to attend this HBU on a full band scholarship, some might say that I squandered it by seeking an alternative path. They may be right, but I don't regret having served this country for twenty-four years one bit.

Let me regress for a minute and go back to my college years. You have to understand that being in a historically black college marching band requires a bit of an initiation that I probably was not ready to undergo. This included things such as:

- pushup cutaways (modified pushups where you land on your chest by throwing out your arms) at 4:00 a.m.;
- running the track and bleachers, then being advised that if you were caught by the Section Leader, you would start all over again (and oh, did I happen to mention that he was a track star?);
- being labeled a "crab" and having to follow the instructions of your upper classmen regardless of the request; and
- having your head shaved.

Well, guess what? At that time in my life, that was not exactly my cup of tea, so I made the decision to join the United States Air Force. Unbeknownst to me, I would undergo an initiation very similar to the one I had just left. You might call this going from the frying pan into the fire.

Having enlisted for four years, my very first day was a rude awakening, yet one that I now was contractually bound to complete. If you have never experienced basic training, let me tell you that it was an emotional and physical shock to my mental well-being. Yet, I managed to succeed and complete basic training six weeks later, along with many others who had started in Flight 2709 on November 14, 1972 at Lackland Air Force Base (AFB), the home of Basic Military Training (BMT) for the US Air Force. Hurrah!

I was not to leave Lackland AFB for many months to come. I was merely shipped across the base to the Security Police Academy (or as it is referred to today, the Security Forces Academy) to complete my technical training as a Security Police Specialist. Approximately seven weeks later, if I recall correctly, I graduated from this technical school without encountering any bumps along the road.

I remained assigned to Lackland AFB because during that time the Vietnam War was still going strong. I knew that if I were to be shipped to Vietnam, I had better have my act together if I wanted to return to the US of A in one piece and in anything other than a body bag. I also knew that there was one creature that the Viet Cong feared and whose senses were much better than most: the Military Working Dog (MWD), or K-9, so I volunteered for the MWD program and was accepted.

I successfully completed the program in approximately twelve weeks without any permanent teeth marks and with a companion whose sense of smell, hearing, and sight were at least ten times better than mine. I now had a tactical advantage should I set foot in Vietnam. I later learned that the Viet Cong had a bounty for MWD handlers and their dogs. Call it the will to survive or merely making sure that I had an advantage going in, but it would prove to be one of the most logical decisions that I had made thus far.

Finally, in the summer of 1973, I received my first assignment and was on my way to Barksdale AFB in Louisiana, home of the 2nd Bomb Wing, the oldest Wing in the Air Force. The funny part was that when I arrived, there were very few B-52 bombers or KC 135 refueling aircraft on station. My inquiry as to why resulted in a "be glad" attitude which I would later understand when most of them returned from their deployment in Guam.

This being my first assignment, I found that my training was to continue before I eventually performed both security and law enforcement duties as an MWD handler. During this training period, I learned a very valuable lesson, only one of many more to follow. This lesson was that the GAU, a shorter version of the M-16 rifle and standard issue for MWD handlers, was my best friend, and I needed to treat it with respect. In order to do this, I needed not only to be able to fire the weapon, but also to be able to disassemble and reassemble it in the dark, which practically meant in my sleep. You are probably wondering why. Well, along with the MWD, this was an instrument—much like the saxophone I had mastered in high school—which could (or should I say, would) save my life in the right situation. Therefore, I learned to do just that. This was an invaluable educational lesson.

Although this was my first assignment, it was not uneventful. I learned that I would not only be handling a MWD, but I would also be handing a bomb detection dog. I seemed to end up in some pretty precarious situations professionally. The first of these was when I was working law enforcement duty and responded to the Enlisted Club due to an altercation that was taking place. This being my first encounter, I relied on the training provided, as well as the MWD.

I soon learned that if you want to get people's attention right away and you have a MWD (Ron was his name) with stainless steel teeth, just let the MWD be the attention getter for you; instantly, any altercation that is going on will cease. Everyone is more focused on exiting the premises or finding higher ground away from those teeth. Result: problem solved and lesson learned. Life should be this easy. Although there were many other encounters, there is nothing like your first one.

On the security side of the house, we provided security in a weapons storage area that one might consider one of the most secure facilities on the installation; it *was* secure, with the exception of the mosquitoes. Those blood-sucking creatures could make your night on patrol a nightmare. You generously applied mosquito repellent to every part of uncovered flesh on your body.

Besides augmenting security during exercises, the duty was good as I continued to learn. And learn I did when the aircraft returned from Guam. The experience of standing guard on a B-52 Stratofortress (a long-range, subsonic, jet-powered strategic bomber) could have been a real treat of boredom. After my first stint guarding one of these mammoth beasts, I could tell you how many bolts and rivets went into manufacturing this aircraft. You constantly had to be vigilant to not let boredom creep in during your normal eight-hour shift (twelve hours during an Air Force inspection team visit or alert).

Many of my fellow security policemen were receiving assignments to the Far East, and I really wanted to go serve. Unfortunately, having the desire to fight for one's country doesn't mean that's the way it will turn out. With less than two years on station, I received an assignment. Not the Far East one that I had hoped for, but to Royal Air Force (RAF) Alconbury in Great Britain. Now you're probably thinking, "What's so bad about that?" Absolutely nothing. At least we spoke the same language, or so I thought, and we weren't at war with Great Britain.

As it turned out, it was an assignment where "I would cut my teeth," as the saying goes. In fact, securing priority resources and aircraft was to prove to be another adventure. Having to learn new skills as an alarm monitor and finally as a communication plotter in Central Security Control, I became very adept at handling crises in a calm and professional manner. We were being tested by either an Air Force Inspection Team or North Atlantic Treaty Organization (NATO) Inspection Team on what sometimes felt like a continual basis.

This is where I did hit a bump in the road when it came to religion and the military. How could I be expected to take someone's life when religion had taught me, "Thou shall not kill"? I found the answer to this question on the basketball court, of all places. During one of the many games we played in the gym/physical fitness facility, one of the individuals I was playing against was the base chaplain. This opportunity allowed me to consult with him, and he explained it to me in such a manner that it was no longer a burning issue in my soul.

On RAF Alconbury, as on many of the bases in Europe at the time, there were protests against deploying the Ground Launch Cruise Missile (GLCM) in Europe. Coupling this with the bombings by terrorist organizations made for increased, continual vigilance on the part of Security Forces. Working with individuals for whom this was an everyday occurrence allowed lifelong comradeships to develop. A keener sense of surroundings, both on and off the installation, was required. I did not sit with my back to the door. When I try to sit near a glass window, I am constantly assessing my surroundings and what to do "just in case" something happens. Another few life lessons well learned.

The most tragic incident was the crash of an airplane that was loaded with civilians and military personnel. The smell of burning flesh and the tremendous amount of twisted metal and smell of fuel is forever engraved in my memory as well as my senses. People coped with this in many different ways. A few never made it past this tragic series of events.

Fortunately, I was selected to work in the Security Forces Training Section, where I learned a significant amount from one of the best supervisors that I have ever had. This ultimately resulted in my becoming an expert in training and developing people. After a couple of years, I was selected to work in the Information and Industrial Security Section. This section handled the initiation of security background checks for clearances and protection of classified information, which was critical to the success of our mission.

During these maturing years, one thing came to mind through the encouragement of my supervisors and the observation of others: I needed to get my formal education off the ground and in gear. I hightailed it over to the Base Education Office to discuss this with a counselor. It just so happened that she was the University of Maryland counselor, the wife of a good friend of mine who pointed me in the right direction. I had no idea of how far up the education ladder I should aspire to climb, but she informed me that the sky was the limit and that I should indicate that PhD was what I wanted to achieve eventually.

So, starting out with the basic courses, I spent many an evening, as well as weekends, in class enriching my mind for greater opportunities. Mind you, I was also learning many lessons in life, as well. I went on to complete the basic undergraduate courses through the University of Maryland during my freshman and sophomore years in England. In addition, I completed other professional leadership courses (e.g., Noncommissioned Officer [NCO] Academy and other technical training courses).

Having spent almost eight years in Great Britain, I returned to the States with a bit of culture shock. You see, in Europe, African Americans were embraced, much more so than in the United States at the time. In addition, the lifestyle was much different and there had been many changes since I had left the States. Just to name a few:

- Technological changes;
- Availability of different types of fast food restaurants (i.e., Wendy's);
- Adjusting to driving on the right side of the road again.

Returning to the States, I was excited to learn that I would be assigned to the Security Police Academy. Well, as luck would have it, I received a telegram while on vacation that I was being diverted to Minot, North Dakota. Okay, was somebody playing a cruel joke on me? Well, as they say, "Everything happens for a reason." Being at Minot Air Force was another eye-opening experience for me. I learned that I would be assigned to the 92nd Missile Security Squadron. Being a part of the Security Police Group that would go on to win the most Outstanding Unit award was in itself a blessing. Having never worked missile security before, I was to receive invaluable training in what this entailed.

Being a Flight Security Supervisor in the missile field is a whole new experience. You work three days on a twelve-hour or longer shift, depending on the circumstances taking place in the missile field. Let me state this as a fact: if this had been my first assignment, I know that I would have had a very short-lived career in the United States Air Force. I can honestly say that I prayed that I would not get used to the extreme climatic conditions in that part of the country. Here again, everything happens for a reason.

The one thing that I did take advantage of was the opportunity to continue my education by attending Minot State University. With the time afforded me over the breaks from the missile field, I was able to complete my junior year of college and obtain an associate's degree in criminal justice. During my time there, I learned many things that were to prove beneficial later in my career.

During my second and final year in North Dakota, I was selected to work in Wing Security Control. This was an assignment that I relished, one that helped me to think on my feet. A few of the people working with me were also working on completing their education. Some were CLEPing many of the courses they needed, shortening the time needed to complete their degrees, but I personally felt that classroom interaction was more beneficial to me in pursuing my studies. Because it provided me with the opportunity to hear and express different points of view, I found it to be more rewarding.

Leaving that frozen part of the world, where temperatures often were below what I believed was humanly possible to exist in, was a welcome relief for me. That summer, I returned to the Security Police Academy, where I was assigned to Camp Bullis as a Course Chief for the Air Base Ground Defense Course. I went through the Academic Instructor course (and many others) on my way to obtaining my Master Instructor certification, and I took a few classes that eventually resulted in my receiving an associate's degree in both Industrial Security and Instructor Technology.

Having served my time at Camp Bullis, I was selected to develop the HMMWV (High Mobility Multi-Purpose Wheeled Vehicle, or Hummer, as they are referred to today) Training Course. Then I was off to Detroit, MI for training at General Motors for this vehicle. Later, I came back to Lackland to train the trainers on the HMMWV.

After completing that task, I went on to teach new officers in the Basic Officers Course, and subsequently I took over as the Superintendent for the Advanced Security Police Courses as well as the Basic Security Police Course. During this period, we were in the process of developing arms control treaties with other countries, and I was fortunate to be one of three selected to be a part of a team recruited by the On-Site Inspection Agency to help carry out the verification process outlined in the treaties—primarily between the former Soviet Union and the United States. Here again, my background and education played a significant role in my selection for the team.

Assigned to the Washington Field Office in Washington DC, I traveled between Texas and DC for a couple of years until I was asked to relocate to the Washington Field Office at Buzzards Point (Coast Guard Headquarters), and later to a more permanent office at Dulles International Airport. My education continued with training at the Defense Intelligence Agency, along with other governmental and civilian agencies, to ensure that I was fully aware of the treaty requirements and procedures.

This proved to be one of the most challenging and rewarding assignments that I had had up to that point in my career. My formal academic education had to be put on hold, since I was required to be ready for deployment at a moment's notice, yet I was being educated in a most unique manner, in ways that I could never have thought. If someone had informed me that I would be taking classes and understanding rocket propulsion, yet alone enjoying the classes, I probably would have said, sarcastically, "Right!" In fact, my education was being enhanced by classes of this nature, along with the many others that I took that gave me the understanding of a new language of diplomacy.

This actually gave me a new appreciation and opened my eyes to being aware of the many different cultural aspects of other countries. Having been in places where people never even saw an African American before, I was actively engaging with people on different levels, even inviting exchange students into our home to share in the American culture while we learned from them as well. Looking back on this, I can really see the advances that we have made as a society, from a technological standpoint to a cultural awareness perspective.

As good fortune would have it, my next selection was one of those that, when the door opens, you had best be prepared to enter it, because it might not open again. Not that the previous assignment was not that way, but this one would take into account everything that I had learned and encountered, and would afford me the opportunity to make a difference for others.

When the position of Command Chief for the Air Force District of Washington (AFDW) became available, I interviewed for the job (along with several others), and was honored to be selected. This position provided me with opportunities to help others while advising the AFDW Commander on the welfare, training, and morale of the more than thirty thousand enlisted individuals we supported in the Washington DC area and deployed around the world. In addition, I was able to advise on the training and welfare needs for the total enlisted force.

This was a daunting task, but I relished the opportunity to accept this new role. Since I was to be the role model for the Enlisted Force, I knew that education now took on even a more important role, not only for me to be able to do my job effectively, but also to provide others with the incentive to continue their education. How was I going to be able to speak at professional military education academies and civic groups if I did not have the credentials to back me up?

Another incentive was that I knew after four more years in this assignment, I would be looking at retiring from the Air Force with twenty-four years of service to our country, and in order to make the transition into the civilian community as a professional, I would need to have my bachelor's degree.

The task was an enormous undertaking, considering that I was now working a forty- to sixty-hour workweek. So again, I found myself at the Education Office seeking a school that would accept the credits I had already obtained and allow me to complete my undergraduate degree. National-Louis University provided just the structured program that I needed to complete my undergraduate degree.

NLU and I developed a road map to make it possible. I buckled down and took weekend classes, spending weekends in class and bugging the wife at 4:00 or 5:00 a.m. to proofread a paper that was due for class that day. Through many long nights, early mornings, and weekends in school, I was able to complete my bachelor's degree with honors. Twenty-some years after I had started, with more worldly experiences and my share of peaks and valleys, I had finally achieved one of the many milestones that I had set out to achieve. The lesson I learned is that, no matter how long it takes, and no matter the obstacles that you may encounter, anything that you set your mind to achieving—you can!

One of the best pieces of advice I received was to take the time and decompress from being in the military before making the leap into the civilian community. As I made that transition, I took up with an upstart company that was progressing from the East Coast toward the West: CarMax, a company that sells previously owned vehicles after taking them through a quality inspection.

I started as a finance manager with CarMax, applying knowledge that I had not used in twenty-plus years, like how to calculate percentages. After demonstrating that I had the ability to sell cars and run a team of successful sales associates, I was later promoted to Customer Service Manager, and then to Sales Manager. Here again, things that I had learned at the universities and military academies came in useful, as I went before boards and was tasked with various exercises, such as the in-basket exercise. For those of you who have never done this before, you're tasked with sorting through an in-basket and identifying the items that need to be worked first, based on their priority.

Good fortune smiled down on me, and I was asked if I would be interested in relocating from Houston to San Antonio. I jumped at the opportunity and challenge of opening a new store and hiring my own team. As one of several sales managers, we worked rotating shifts that did not allow much time for continued education. Although I received formal training through CarMax, after being with the company for a couple of years, I still had that burning desire to complete my graduate degree. As Anthony D'Angelo once said, "Develop a passion for learning. If you do, you will never cease to grow."

Thus began another chapter in my life. I can hear my mother saying, "Sometimes it's not what you know, but who you know." That proved to be true when one day, as I waited with several others to board the buses heading to a Dallas Cowboys football game, I happened to run into an individual I had worked with in Washington, DC. If you remember, my first aspiration was to achieve my PhD. That desire burned even more intensely after speaking with him.

I saw that there just might be an opportunity, if I could land a job with CPS Energy, to achieve that goal. I was successful in obtaining a project analyst position in the Facilities, Security and Maintenance Division. Fortunately, I still had some of my GI Bill left to continue my education, and after proving I was up to the challenge, I decided that it was time for me to locate a university where I could attend classes at night and on weekends. I guess I am just a glutton for punishment. However, as the saying goes, anything that is worth having is worth making a few sacrifices for in order to achieve it.

Seeking out the best option, I discovered that Webster University had a master's program that I was interested in pursuing—a dual major in Management and Human Resource Development. Although it might take a little longer, it would be worth it in the end. After completing this program opportunities started to come my way at work, and I progressed up the corporate ladder to a new position approximately every two years.

I retired from CPS Energy after managing the Diversity and Inclusion program. Shortly after that, I was offered the opportunity to apply for a position at the University of Texas at San Antonio (UTSA). I interviewed and accepted the job as the Career Counselor for the College of Engineering. It was almost as if I had come full circle. Once again, I had the opportunity to give back through my years of experience, helping others as they start down their own path in life.

Oh, the joy of education! What a thrill it has been as I look back over the years, seeing where I started and where I have ended up. I am only two-thirds of the way there, but I am beginning to think I have achieved my journey in a different way. Based on the schools I have attended (and there have been many), along with the experiences I gained—the many peaks and valleys, coupled with the many destinations to which I have traveled and in which I have lived—I feel as if I have achieved a PhD in life. I would not trade it for all the riches in the world, because this journey is not over yet; I'm just waiting for the next door to open, and open it will in due time. I just need to make sure that I am ready when that door opens.

The lesson that I have learned is that if you expect life to be great, learn from every experience and have fun doing it, because you're only going to have one crack at it. As Maya Angelou said, "When you know better, you do better." I have known all along that I could do better, and the years have proved this to be true. Education is the heart of our society, and at the heart of an education are new opportunities to make a difference for others.

JOHN LEE
AIR FORCE

As a longtime writing instructor at the University of Texas at San Antonio (UTSA), John Lee was an inspiration to hundreds of students, urging them to accept responsibility for their own lives and to learn how to effectively express themselves in writing.

So, you're in my university freshman composition class. And you're a vet. Great. So am I. We should have some shared experiences. However, there's a good chance you were what we called a grunt (Army combat), while I was an Air Force medic on an air base in Saigon during 1969. I took care of a lot of grunts in the Air Evac unit I worked at when I first arrived at Tan Son Nhut.

I went to Vietnam right out of tech school. I made it there with less than eight months' service under my belt, including two tech school stints, the first being 90 percent security police (SP) training. However, I was taken out of SP school and transferred to the medical field. I didn't complain a lot, thinking that, with my college and work background, I would end up a paper pusher. Silly me. Actually, I had signed up to be a pilot. However, that's another story, probably one you might also relate with.

So, you're a vet in my class. Understand that you won't get special treatment just because I am a vet and you're a vet. No one gets special treatment, and that's the way it should be. It doesn't matter anyway, because, from my experience, 90 percent or more of the vets whom I have taught have done well in class. Done well does not mean they all received A grades, but most often these vets have been among the best students in the class.

To me, vets doing well only makes sense. This is simply because you will have an advantage over the typical eighteen-year-old in the class with you. Use it. You earned it in more ways than one.

This advantage is no secret. On the first day of class, I tell the eighteen-year-olds about their disadvantage, and tell them they have to overcome it quickly or suffer the consequences. Many won't adjust and will end up with a D or an F. Some will have to sit through Composition I again.

The eighteen-year-olds' disadvantage is that, while they are sitting in my university classroom, they still think they are working under the "rules" of high school. They think I will treat them the same way their high school teachers did, and that they can get away with the same nonsense, like turning in work late, or being guaranteed their lowest scores will be dropped, or the practice of school districts that won't allow a grade lower than fifty on any assignment, or a school principal not allowing a teacher to fail more than one or two students in a class.

You, on the other hand, know damn well you're not in high school. You, on the other hand, have matured, something your fellow freshmen, for the most part, have not done, and may or may not do their first semester. They will splash in a lake of freedom, some drowning. They will be involved in everything social, often to the detriment of grades. Education, for many of them, will be on the back burner at best. Education is the only reason you're here. Advantage you.

At the same time, eighteen-year-olds out on their own for the first time find it hard to get started on tasks like homework or waking up. You, on the other hand, have experience fulfilling commitments, whether someone was watching over you or not. The vets I have worked with, for the most part, have been good workers who put in the sweat needed to improve their writing skills. Many freshmen won't put in the work. Many will be satisfied with a C or a D, even though, with a little work, they could earn a letter grade higher. You won't be satisfied with less than your best effort. Advantage you.

Additionally, one of the hardest lessons for freshmen to learn is paying attention to detail, especially little details that make or break an essay's grade. I am sure they think I am a nit-picking bastard. So be it. I tell them there are jobs (EMT or soldier) and pastimes (flying or mountain climbing) where a lack of paying attention to detail can result in death. I tell them that a corporation is also adamant about detail, even more so, since screwing up details can cost them money, and they really don't like losing money.

Paying attention to detail should be no stranger to you, no matter your service MOS. If I hadn't learned this simple fact as a reporter before volunteering in 1968, I sure learned it in basic training from my drill instructor, who was on my case big time. I couldn't figure out why he went out of his way to give me a hard time, but later found out drill instructors jumped on two types of potential trouble makers: juvenile delinquents and college graduates, of which I was the latter. To this day, I clean house in places no normal person would even look.

Another major problem freshmen have, a carryover from high school, is an inability to follow instructions. I will spend all semester telling many of them to do "X" and they will never do it, even after losing points for not doing it on three or four papers. A simple task of turning in copies of all sources, for instance, will never get done.

Following instructions will be a breeze for you after following, or even giving, orders in the service for years. You realize there is a reason for them, even if it is only to see how well they are carried out.

Returning to an earlier point, you may have noted: when I went to school on the GI Bill, I was attending graduate school, so I had experience going to college. Actually, I had attended two universities. However, there is still a lesson for you in this. It has to do with maturity, a point made earlier.

When I was an undergrad, I worked a minimum of thirty-eight hours a week, and, during my senior year, up to sixty hours in two different states, requiring a goodly amount of commuting each day. My day during my senior year started at 5:00 a.m. and ended at about midnight. I was taking a full load of classes, working, chasing women, and racing sports cars during most of college. As a result, I graduated with something like a 2.2 GPA.

It also took me five years to graduate, a smart move during the Vietnam War. I was even drafted my senior year, but had it nullified with the help of my university, since the draft board wasn't allowed to draft a full-time college student close to graduation. That was why I volunteered for the Air Force a couple of months or so before graduation, especially since I had qualified to be a pilot, the only way a non- ROTC college grad could get into the service in 1968.

After my service, I got married, and following a stint working for my parents, I decided to go back to school on the GI Bill to get a bachelor's degree in journalism. However, I was surprisingly accepted on a trial basis to graduate school. This was only due to a graduate advisor and professor who believed that people change over time and that I wasn't still the 2.2 GPA student I had been prior to being in the service.

Graduate school applicants were supposed to have a minimum 3.0 GPA. Luckily, he gave me a chance and let me in based on my journalism work experience. I doubt anyone else would have. Later, he told me he thought I wasn't going to last two weeks. Surprised, to say the least, I asked, "Why did you do it, then?" He replied, "I always give a student a chance."

I went on past the master's work and completed all the course work for a doctorate and, a few years later, the course work for another master's at yet another university, accumulating a GPA of around 3.80 over more than one hundred hours of graduate work. How did a 2.2 GPA undergrad do that? Maturity. Maturity gained in the service, a war, marriage, and the birth of a son had made me a new, serious man. Well, more than I had been. I was still racing cars, and I learned to fly in my own plane, thanks to having been hired as a full-time writer for the university while going to school on the GI Bill.

You bring maturity and real-world experience to your university and your classes. This is an advantage most of the eighteen-year-olds in your classes won't gain without some pain of their own during their first semester, or even, in some cases, their first year. I am not saying that this transfer to university life will be easy, nor will getting great grades in my class. Set your sights on improving each new assignment. Learn. That's what we do here.

This reminds me of a saying a longtime friend (and two-Vietnam-tour career Army officer) and I had when dealing with what we thought was going to be a simple, quickly resolved problem on a race car. After working hours on what we had figured was a twenty-minute problem, we'd look at each other and laughingly say, "*Nothing* is easy," and then we'd go have a cold drink with a feeling of pride in our accomplishment, no matter how small it was.

JEFF GATLIN
USAF, ASSISTANT DIRECTOR, UTSA COUNSELING CENTER

Jeff is known across campus as the "go-to" person in counseling. If you have a student you don't know how to help, a situation you don't know what to do about, or a student group that needs a speaker, he is always there. Time and again I have talked student veterans in to going to "talk to him for a few minutes," only to have them come back later to tell me what a difference he has made in their lives. We are lucky to have him on campus as a resource for student veterans.

"We Don't Need Another Hero," the song, has been running through my head since 2005—about nine years now. It's a great song, but I'm pretty fucking tired of it. For those of you too young to remember, it was part of the soundtrack to the 1985 movie, *Mad Max—Beyond Thunderdome*. Tina Turner, in the form of her awkwardly named character, Aunty Entity, sings of the fragility of individual human beings—heroes—in the face of war.

In 2005, I had been working at UTSA for three years when I met Harold. He had an old man's name but he was a freshman in college. He told me that he had served one thirteen-month tour in Vietnam. "Marines did thirteen months, the Army only did twelve," he said. During intake, Harold reported that he had spent most of his time in Phu Bai. This would have been in 1965 or 1966. His graying ponytail indicated that he was well past his physical prime. But he was still a Marine, and he was still in Vietnam.

We had about thirty sessions together. The general limit for a college counseling center is twelve, but it wouldn't have made any difference if we had met a hundred times. Harold had been living with untreated PTSD for forty years. Well, it was untreated in the sense that he had never spoken to a mental health professional about his time in Vietnam. On the other hand, he had one hell of a drug regimen that seemed to be keeping him functional. He had been smoking marijuana forever, and he regularly consumed amphetamines, mescaline, cocaine in its various forms, and he drank all the alcohol his liver could handle. During one of our early sessions, he told me that he had "a tendency toward depression and a fuck-it-all attitude." By the time we terminated treatment, *I* was exhibiting a tendency toward depression and a fuck-it-all attitude.

The truth is that I didn't know how to treat PTSD at the time. But neither did anyone else. Harold was in the system, meaning that he had been diagnosed and had a disability rating—for PTSD. But the only treatment he ever received was chemical in nature, most of it supplied by his dealers on the street. His dealers at the VA just couldn't match the potency or the efficiency of the other suppliers.

Harold didn't make it through college. He dropped out after yet another semester on academic probation and an altercation with the chair of the department regarding his fitness for the career he was hoping to go into. In reality, he never had a chance. I was pretty sure he wasn't going to be successful academically. But hell, he survived combat in Vietnam, why couldn't he survive Freshman English?

I'll tell you why. Harold didn't make it through college because he was addicted. He was addicted because he had been suffering from PTSD for about as long as I had been alive. Harold didn't beat the odds because he is not a hero. He is a flesh and blood man who answered the call to serve his country and paid the price for it. Even as he was being dismissed from the university for the last time, and even as he was being denied access to the legitimate occupation he wanted to pursue, he never expressed a sense of sorrow for himself and never referred to himself as a hero.

Since 2005, I've worked with dozens, or scores, or maybe even hundreds of vets. And I have stopped using the word hero. I've come to the conclusion that calling vets "heroes" simply protects us, the civilian population, from the harsh reality that veterans—if they survive their war—continue to suffer through when they return home.

In an article recently published on Salon.com, Cara Hoffman argues that the word "hero" can be "dangerously dismissive." She goes on:

> … "hero" refers to a character, a protagonist, something in fiction, not to a person, and using this word can hurt the very people it's meant to laud. While meant to create a sense of honor, it can also buy silence, prevent discourse and benefit those in power more than those navigating the new terrain of home after combat.

Stop the hero worship. Look at our veterans for who they really are, courageous but fragile men and women who have deliberately chosen to serve their country—the men and women who continue to pay the price, long after their war is over.

LISA FIRMIN

RETIRED AIR FORCE
COLONEL AND
ASSOCIATE PROVOST
OF FACULTY/STUDENT
DIVERSITY AND
RECRUITMENT AT UTSA

If I were asked to describe Colonel Firmin in one word, it would be quick. She walks quickly, talks quickly, and is always on the go. She is quick to smile and praise people, but doesn't put up with laziness or mismanagement. When faced with problems, she wastes no time consulting with all the people involved to find and implement workable solutions. Since coming to UTSA, she has energized our Veterans Services, worked tirelessly to increase the diversity among students, faculty, and staff, and implemented a diversity award program on campus. The combination of a quick mind and the flexibility she developed in the military has made her transition to academia both faster and more impressive than she herself even realizes.

THE TRANSITION: COLONEL TO ASSOCIATE PROVOST

Transitioning from a career in the military to working in higher education is like going from one foreign culture to another. They really are that different. They each have their own ethos, values, manner of dress, and vocabulary. I had a military mindset, can-do attitude, and a strong mission focus, and I thoroughly believed I could transfer my skill set, especially my leadership skills, to the world of academia and make a difference for underserved and nontraditional populations at a Hispanic Serving Institution (HSI).

I mean, how hard could it be to make that transition? After all, I served in countless leadership roles in the military, led large organizations that at one point exceeded 1,600 personnel in seven diverse organizations, oversaw $3.7 billion in infrastructure, was responsible for a $25.6 million budget, served in peacetime and in combat, was a highly decorated veteran, and excelled in austere environments while literally being shot at. So, again, I asked myself, "Just how hard could it be?" Harder than I ever thought it would be!

Here's my story. I joined the military right out of college. I wanted to pay my country back since I had gone to school under my father's GI Bill. I really wanted to be the first in my family to get a college degree and go on to become a leader. The military afforded me that opportunity. Soon after joining, I was in charge of hundreds of troops. The military is good like that: they provide you with the training and then you get out there and perform—it is sink or swim time. Truly an outstanding leadership laboratory made up of real-world experience.

My first assignment was in a traditionally all-male fighter pilot unit (at that time women could not fly fighter aircraft), and I happened to be the first woman officer assigned. After that, I found myself on the flight line in the Philippines among a unit of seven hundred (with only ten women), and I was the only woman officer. I was literally told that the flight line was no place for a woman, so why was I even there? It wasn't the first time that I found myself in a very small minority, and it certainly wasn't the last.

Many times throughout my career in the military, I was the first woman officer assigned to the unit, the first woman commander, the first woman leader—you get the gist. I won't even talk about being the only Latina around for miles. Back in those days and in all those many duty locations I was assigned to, most people had never seen a Latina up close. I truly was a standout. I stood out as a woman *and* as a Latina; everything I did was watched closely, all the time. At least that is what it felt like to me.

I've served as a squadron and group commander for organizations sized from 250 to more than 1,600 personnel, including active duty, civilians, and contractors. This is a true leadership test, as you are responsible for the entire organization—its mission, logistics, production, resources, and personnel—24/7. You are responsible for all this during peacetime and when your organization goes into combat. It is a heavy responsibility that a commander never takes lightly. I certainly never did. I knew that each and every one of my troops was my responsibility.

I was honored to have served with so many outstanding people all over the world. My family moved seventeen times to accommodate all the places the military sent me. That can take its toll on one's family, and I know how hard it was on my husband and son. There were times they made the move by themselves because I had to stay behind or go ahead due to mission requirements. Military family members know about resilience; they live it every day. I was gone a lot, missing quite a few birthdays, anniversaries, and other important events in their lives—all sacrifices made for our country.

Would I do it again? You bet. Why? Because it was a great experience, I believe in my country, and if more of us don't actually serve, what would become of our great nation? I stayed in a long time because I believed I was making a difference and that I had an impact on people's lives. Despite all the sacrifices, I learned a lot about myself, about leadership, and about others in their best of times and in their worst of times. I am a better person for having served.

Most people want to know how I found myself in higher education and in my current role as Associate Provost. It sort of just fell into place. Remember that old saying: "Bloom where you are planted"? I have always done that, always done my very best at whatever job I had. I was serving as the Air Force ROTC Commander at the University of Texas at San Antonio (UTSA), helping to bring in more students to UTSA and into the Air Force as young lieutenants upon their graduation from college.

This by the way, was a great job match, as I had attended high school in San Antonio, was a Latina from South Texas, and UTSA is a Hispanic Serving Institution. I could definitely relate to many of the students I recruited, mentored, taught, and led. I knew firsthand how important it could be to have a role model that looks like you—something I never had in the military. I didn't work for another woman until I was assigned to the Pentagon after eighteen years in the military, and I never did work for a Latino/a officer. In my role as Commander of UTSA's AF ROTC Detachment 842, I led an outstanding team and detachment to national recognition as the Best Large Detachment in the Air Force in 2009. After that I decided it was time to retire: best to do that on a high note, no?

So my husband and I decided to start putting out feelers via my resume about what would come next, and in doing that, I realized what I *didn't* want to do. I think that is an important exercise to go through—to really learn what it is that you don't want to do. It helps you as you move forward in finding what it is that you *do* want to do. I wanted the next chapter of my life to be about something that I am passionate about.

Before I even really started to think much more about it, I was approached by a military-affiliated agency about working in diversity management. At almost the same time, I was approached by the leadership at UTSA about the possibility of working with them in a leadership role in regards to diversity and recruitment. I did have extensive experience in the military (including at the highest levels at the Pentagon) working recruitment, retention, and diversity. Let me also say that I am passionate about education, diversity, and helping those in underserved populations.

My husband and I gave it a lot of thought and finally determined that UTSA was the place for me, as it combined all my passions into a role where I could truly make a difference. I hung up my uniform and prepared to transition into a newly created role at the university. I do regret not taking more time off to decompress from all those years in the military and prepare myself mentally for the challenge of the transition. I took the executive transition assistance program course that was offered by the military about a year before retiring, but I don't believe it really prepared me for the complete transition that I was about to undergo. I guess the old commander in me felt that since I had already had a successful military career and had seen just about everything, including combat, what more could I face that I wouldn't be prepared for, or could readily adapt to?

I retired after serving in the military for thirty years. That's a long time of never having a first name and always knowing what you are going to wear to work every day. You laugh, but I am serious. There is something to be said for standardization, good order, and discipline on a daily basis; it means never having to worry about the small things. I also like the fact that I don't have to deploy anymore and that I don't have to work twelve-hour shifts unless I want to. My husband says I still work too long and hard. Guess some habits are very hard to break.

I was always called by my rank and last name, or simply "Ma'am." I was only called by my first name on rare occasions, typically by those who outranked me. When I retired as the senior ranking Latina officer in the Air Force, there weren't many who outranked me at a standard operating location. And even though I was a Mrs., no one *ever* called me Mrs.

It took a while to get used to having a first name again. To this day, many still call me Colonel, and you know what? That is fine with me. After all, I earned that title and rank. But it is also okay to be called by my first name, too. That is a good thing that it is okay with me. I know some retired colonels and generals who couldn't make that transition and still insist on being called only by their rank.

You have no idea how hard it was and how uneasy I felt when I began having to select an outfit to wear to work every day. Civilian clothes, what is that? And accessories, what are those? I wore camouflage and combat boots most of the time. I never even carried a purse, and now I had to accessorize! This freaked me out more than actually doing my new job. I knew I could do any job, could lead any initiative, but I couldn't figure out what to wear to work for the first few weeks. It took me an hour or more of staring at my closet each evening just to figure out what to wear the next day.

And shoes—forget about it. I had no idea that professional, nice-looking shoes that were also comfortable were so hard to come by. I longed for my combat boots. I had blisters all over my toes that first week. My husband told me one evening that I was going to have to get better at this civilian clothes thing because I couldn't take an hour or more every day just to figure out what to wear. I will admit that I did buy the wrong clothes before I started working; I should have only bought a few things and started work first to get the lay of the land and determine how people typically dressed in my new environment.

It took me a while. During one presentation early after my transition, I informed the audience that I felt more comfortable in the middle of the Sunni Triangle in Iraq in full body armor than I did standing in front of them wearing these civilian clothes. It wasn't the presentation; it was what I was wearing, and I simply wasn't used to seeing myself as a civilian. I also remember walking by a glass wall, seeing my reflection, and wondering who that civilian was. It takes time, ladies and gentlemen, to shed those thirty years of wearing that uniform. It was almost like I was shedding my first skin. It sort of hurt. I wasn't prepared for the mental transition that I had to go through. No one had ever told me what I would experience.

Higher education, just like the military and a lot of organizations, has its own culture and way of doing business. People assumed that, because I had worked as the AF ROTC commander at UTSA, I knew more about the university than I did. However, I was an AF active duty member at that time and, although I knew some people, I wasn't in the personnel system of the university. I didn't report up through their chain of command, and I didn't really understand their structure and the "why" behind how they got that way. It wasn't obvious to me why certain departments were set up like they were. I know that this can be confusing to many veterans; the higher ed structure doesn't seem logical to us. It can be confusing as to where you go for certain assistance on campus or what office is actually in charge of what as you try to register for classes, learn about your transfer credits, find out about housing, financial aid or scholarships, and on and on.

I certainly didn't understand their multiple uses of acronyms. We in the military used acronyms all the time; I just wasn't aware that they did it as much or more in higher ed. I remember attending several meetings those first few weeks and hearing acronyms, but I had no idea what they were referring to. For example, the Provost was discussing PPE, and I immediately went to Personal Protection Equipment; I was thinking of body armor and other personal protection equipment. Now I knew he wasn't talking about that, but what *was* he talking about? He was talking about Professional Performance Evaluation, but I didn't know that.

Another time, an individual spoke to me about the IED, and I immediately went to Improvised Explosive Device. She wasn't talking about that; she was talking about the Institute for Economic Development. My mind went to where it was most comfortable, and I was sad to say that it went to explosives. What does that say about my experiences and me?

I recall attending the first few meetings on campus. In the military, you are taught to be early and never late. I would rather be one hour early than a minute late. When I arrived at my first few meetings at least ten to fifteen minutes early, the doors were locked, and no one was anywhere in sight. I thought I had the wrong room or the wrong day, but that wasn't the case. At exactly the appointed hour, someone approached the door, unlocked it, and others arrived. Not what I was used to, but now I don't arrive early anymore. I arrive on time.

All these things may seem like very small, trivial things to you, but to me they were not. They were important because they were unknown to me. It was a less structured environment that I wasn't aware of, and I had to learn without the benefit of a handbook, a checklist, a sponsor, or a battle buddy informing me of the ROE (rules of engagement)—things that were routine in the more structured military environment.

Those first few weeks and months were a bit uneasy for me, but no one knew that. I used the skill set I had fine-tuned over many years to be transparent (except for those blisters) and to navigate my way into higher education and build relationships, learn the ropes, and begin to make a difference. I was able to transfer my leadership skills to help the university in its own transformation towards Tier One status.

The collaborations and partnerships I have been able to be engaged in have been absolutely vital in assisting my efforts towards ensuring that diversity and recruitment initiatives are, and continue to be, successful. It has been a great experience to seek out diversity champions and work alongside them for the greater good of our students and faculty. There are many outstanding faculty, staff, and students who care and are ready to jump in and do the work on behalf of the students we serve.

One nontraditional population we serve is our veteran students. I serve as cochair of the Veteran Services Advisory Committee (VSAC) along with the Director of our Career Center (also a vet). Together we lead an outstanding group of individuals from across the campus that includes the President's Military Liaison; personnel from the Veteran Certification Office, Registrar, Advising, Faculty, Disability Services, Counseling Services, and the Student Veteran Association (SVA); and our VetSuccess on Campus counselors (Department of Veteran Affairs employees).

We worked long and hard to coordinate with the Department of Veterans Affairs to be able to have two of their employees on our campus as part of the VetSuccess on Campus program. One of the most significant milestones on our campus in regards to veteran support was the day in 2012 when the Memorandum of Understanding was signed by both the VA and UTSA, paving the way for their vocational counselors to become part of our support network to assist student veterans.

The VSAC's mission is to assist veterans in making a seamless transition from military service to our academic community at UTSA. We recognize the unique experiences that student veterans bring to our campus environment and leverage these resources to help steer our student veterans toward degree, certificate, or program completion by providing a welcoming and helpful support system. We have a four-pronged approach to our support: the robust, collaborative nature of our VSAC, our strong Veteran Certification office, the vibrant students in the SVA, and the experienced VetSuccess counselors.

A wonderful example of collaboration was during the government shutdown in 2013. We were concerned that the longer the shutdown went on, the greater the potential was for some of our student veterans to fail to receive part or all of their benefits. Some of our students informed us of hardships that would occur, affecting housing and, potentially, their tuition and fees. So we pulled together a contingency plan that organized not only the four key prongs of support, but also many other offices and departments across campus, like housing, child care, and fiscal services—all to ensure that our student vets would not have to go without. Although the government shutdown did not last long enough for us to fully implement our plan, we were ready. I was extremely proud of the way UTSA pulled together in support of student veterans.

On another occasion, the VSAC and the Registrar's office worked together with the VetSuccess counselors to ensure a student veteran did not get evicted from a local apartment complex because he hadn't received his federal VA benefits in a timely manner. There are countless more examples of how we as a university pull together on a daily basis to ensure that our student vets receive the care and attention they need so they can concentrate on doing well in their educational programs and graduate.

Even our faculty gets into the act when it comes to supporting our student vets. A faculty member referred a Marine veteran student to my office because the student had apparently stopped contributing in the classroom and wasn't responding to the faculty member's outreach. Initially the student was reluctant to visit with me, but after a time he did come by. Once we determined that we had both served in Iraq at the same time, we began to bond, and he started to let me know what was bothering him: several of his fellow Marines had died in combat, and others had recently committed suicide.

Understandably, he was having a hard time coping with this. I was able to assist him by being there, speaking with him, personally relating to his experience, and referring him to several other areas, one of which was the Student Veteran Association. As soon as I contacted their president, they made contact with him. That is what we do here at UTSA: we step in and assist our students in whatever way we can to ease their transition to higher ed and in the ultimate successful completion of their educational program.

In 2013, I had the good fortune, along with colleagues from the Department of Labor and UTSA's Office of Institutional Research, to present at the annual conference of the American Association of Hispanics in Higher Education. We presented a preconference workshop entitled "Serving the Veteran Population in Higher Education." This was a national-level look at the veteran population and an overview of how UTSA is purposefully meeting the needs of the veteran student. We shared with our colleagues how UTSA was using the four-pronged approach (VSAC, Vet Cert Office, SVA, and VetSuccess counselors) to provide top-notch support to our student veterans.

I would like to point out one particular subcommittee that we have formed under the VSAC that focuses on veteran cultural competence. We understand that the veteran culture is different from the higher ed environment. We want to ensure that both our faculty and staff understand the nuances of these differences, so we prepared a presentation, entitled "Adapt and Overcome: Helping Student Veterans Transition to Academic Life" for the annual Student Affairs Conference, and we also presented it to staff and student employees to help them understand more about our veteran population at UTSA. Further, in our continuous improvement efforts, we've taken that presentation and adapted it to an online educational training module that has been tailored for faculty.

As you can see, my colleagues and I care about helping others. I especially do when I can combine that with education and assisting those in underserved populations. Sometimes others need me to be their voice at the table and advocate on their behalf. Since I too am a veteran, assisting this particular population has been a natural and appropriate fit for me. I no longer feel uneasy about not wearing a uniform, but I will never forget what wearing the uniform felt like and why I wore it for so long. This is why I know I must do whatever I can to help my fellow veterans succeed at UTSA.

5

CIVILIANS: WORKING TO HELP VETERANS SUCCEED IN COLLEGE

AARON CASSIL
PROFESSOR AT UTSA

When I met Aaron we were both PhD Students at the University of California San Diego. Twenty-seven years later, we have been married for twenty-five years, are both professors at the University of Texas at San Antonio, have twin daughters who just graduated from UT Austin, and even say "y'all" sometimes. Aaron is an award-winning Professor at UTSA who has won both the prestigious Piper Teaching Award and the University of Texas Systems Regents Outstanding Teaching Award, and he is the Principle Investigator on multiple grants supporting STEM (Science, Technology, Engineering, and Mathematics) education at UTSA.

If you were to ask me about my strangest conversations with students, it would have to be the ones I've had with vets. I've had lots of students ask me about DNA structure and mitosis, about career choices, research projects, and even problems with roommates or dating. Those are all experiences I have trained for and gone through myself, and I have some clear ideas on what to do and how to handle the situation. But vets bring in a completely different reality. I've had many students seeking extra time on exams because they have ADHD or test anxiety, but only one who suffered a severe head injury when his Humvee was blown up driving down a dirt road and his two buddies were just gone in an instant. This is a world I'd never prepared for, never even dreamed existed while I slaved my way through Ivy League undergraduate and prestigious PhD programs. I know what it is like to have a department chair who wants to end your career or a thesis advisor who is trying to squeeze one more publication out of you, but never have I dealt with a shadowy terrorist group putting a bounty on my life or a commander pressuring me to figure out where the enemy might be hiding as fellow soldiers were dying because I wasn't coming up with an answer.

These were all dramatic stories. But none of them were told to me as teary or choked-up traumatic readings or as ploys for extra points or as tales of prowess that put the students in a special standing. This was just their reality, and it had come into the world of academics. Although they don't ask for it, I always feel like I need to give them some special treatment. But I think they actually want something different—for their world to be normal, a place where they wouldn't be viewed as an oddity, something to be naturally worried about. So this is an additional concern. The situation is different than the norm, but the best service is to treat it as if it isn't.

But even though we join many other Americans in honoring the service of veterans, there is often some level of tension. There seems to be a natural antipathy between faculty and vets. Some of this is based on stereotypes: faculty will be liberals; vets will be right-wingers; faculty will want open questioning of things; vets will want specifics; faculty want to go slow; vets want to charge in. But perhaps some of this is an odd collision of two groups who want to be recognized for the good they do but have trouble recognizing it in each other.

Imagine two brothers who were raised to serve and assist their fellow citizens, but each in a different way. One is very physically oriented, providing protection and building security around people. The other is oriented towards thinking about how to make lives better and communicating to people how to change themselves. One might think that these brothers would find a synergy from their different approaches and would bond together over their interest in helping others. But in this case, these two have developed suspicion, and even resentment, about each other. This is the strange contradiction in the interplay of academia and the military. Both groups are made up of people who have made sacrifices to be in a place where they can earn the satisfaction of serving others, but they don't always see that in each other. This misunderstanding leads to tension and sometimes even frustration and resentment. Maybe by opening up and acknowledging the differences and valuing both types of sacrifice, both groups can learn to help each other.

The deprivations military personnel go through are often displayed in the media. At the same time, many articles have depicted professors as having a soft and easy life. Stress is something they hand out to students, work time is limited, and the long, lazy summer is just an extended vacation. But if this is such a paradise job, why doesn't everyone sign up?

First comes four years of doing well as an undergraduate, then the strain of graduate school. My PhD took me six and a half years of year-round attendance, which is the average for a biology degree. Most of this was spent working with radioactivity and hazardous chemicals in a lab, repeating experiments over and over again until the data was consistent and made sense. It also included lots of grunt work: washing dishes, racking test tubes, and grading papers. Like the military, a lot of the work gets done by people who earn very little but like the job. I received a generous stipend of $7,000 per year while in graduate school, which went up to $21,000 for my four years of post-doc work.

What is a post-doc? After getting a biology PhD, you still can't get a faculty position. You need to spend an average of five more years working in a lab—ten to twelve hours a day, six to seven days a week—before you can apply for a faculty job. And getting that job is no shoo-in. Most tenure-track positions have fifty to two hundred applicants. I applied to forty-five positions to get seven interviews that resulted in three offers. I took a position paying $40,000/yr with the option of making $12,000 more if I could find additional research grant support.

I had little choice about the location. While most cities have a university, there are usually only a handful of openings each year, and the departments may be looking for a very specific subspecialty. My wife's family wanted us to live in California. My family wanted the Seattle area. My choices were Youngstown, Norfolk, or San Antonio. Like many military families, we went where the job sent us and bloomed where we were planted. Many academics do their undergrad, grad, post-doc, and faculty positions in different cities, moving every few years like many military personnel. Growing roots and staying close to family is essentially impossible.

At thirty-five, I had my first real job and a brand new family. Kids had to wait until there was some sort of security. But there really wasn't security, yet. I was an assistant professor. I had five years to publish enough papers, win enough grant support, serve on enough committees, and teach well enough to earn tenure. Failure in any one of these categories meant a one-year terminal contract and going back out to compete with the ever-enlarging horde of candidates trying to get the ring.

Academic home life is not an automatic paradise. The hours are flexible, but, like military service, the demands never end. There is always one more experiment to do, one more paper to read, one more lecture to improve, one more exam to grade, one more student wanting advice, one more grant to submit, one more rejection to overcome. When final grades go in, it isn't time to kick back but a break when you can spend all your time in the lab. They say that military spouses can feel deserted as their loved ones sign up for another round of duty and missions that they don't understand. The same can happen to academics. Why go back to the lab to add nutrients to plates of monkey cells when you could stay home and help with the kids? Why spend another weekend trying to rephrase the grant you've already spent two months on?

Finally, at the age of forty-two, I received tenure. This is a comfortable place, and many think that this is where the posh life begins. But the chance of getting to this level is low. Only one-quarter of the professors in the US have tenure. Like the military—where only a certain group get past major—academics can cut you off in the middle of what you think is a promising career. The majority of the teachers you may encounter are adjunct faculty. Their teaching assignments are given out semester by semester, and they can be terminated at any time. Some of these positions pay as little as $25,000 per year, even with a graduate degree.

To make ends meet, some faculty work at two or more universities, driving back and forth between campuses. Some faculty do rise to the top and have six-figure salaries, but many put in endless hours for limited pay. Just like the military, we can look at our version of full-bird colonels and generals and talk about how they have it made, but there are a lot of people who don't get the salary and perks and work because they love being responsible for helping students help themselves to achieve their goals.

And the idea of sitting around is a myth. Faculty are among the most judged employees in the world. Our teaching is evaluated by surveys and observations every semester. Our research is reviewed by peers before it can be published, and grants go through such a strenuous review that only 10–15 percent of them are funded. We are continuously informed by administrators, peers, and students that we aren't doing our job to their standards.

Obviously, this doesn't compare with the terrible stories I outlined in the opening, and I am not trying to push competition. Rather, I would hope that both groups can come to appreciate each other more and realize that they share a common ground of service that improves our country. Both are looking for positive ideals of freedom, just in different ways. Both have gone through trials and deprivations to be in a place where they could help others.

Maybe we can help each other to accomplish those goals if we spend more time being aware of the similarities and not the differences of that service. Maybe faculty can appreciate the frustrations that many vets feel if they realize the common origins of the need to serve and don't dwell on the difference in approach. Maybe vets can feel more connected to academia if they realize that it isn't just a soft path for people who don't want to work; it is a calling to serve that has its own sets of sacrifices and actually has some core elements in common with their own path.

DIANNE HENGST

DIRECTOR OF STUDENT DISABILITY SERVICES AT UTSA

In the few short years she has been at UTSA, Dianne has had a major impact on our Student Disability Services, and on the campus as a whole. As a Clinical Psychologist herself, she brings a calm confidence to helping everyone, from students striving to succeed at UTSA despite physical and psychological issues to faculty trying to figure out how best to help them do so. Under her leadership, more of our veteran students are receiving disability assistance than ever before, and their academic accomplishments attest to the value of the services she has introduced and championed.

As the demographics in college admissions expand, there is greater diversity in today's college classroom (Davis, 1993). Today's typical classroom might include students whose first language is not English; students who are not reading at the same level; students with attention and motivational problems; students from varied cultural backgrounds; students with different learning styles; and students who are gifted (Rose & Meyer, 2002; Council for Exceptional Children, 2005). Furthermore, because the definition of diversity in higher education includes those students who are historically underrepresented, students with disabilities should be considered as part of that diverse student population. Rothstein (1991) indicated that between 1980 and 1990, the number of disabled students attending institutions of higher education had tripled. Today, the US Department of Education estimates that more than 10 percent of entering college freshmen have some type of disability.

In the last ten years, part of the increase of students with disabilities in higher education is due to the rising number of veterans with disabilities. In a May 2012 Huffington Post article, Marilyn Marchione wrote that many post-9/11 veterans returning from combat include veterans with disabilities. Marchione indicated that 1600 of those veterans have lost at least one limb; 156 of them are blind; more than 177,000 of them have a hearing loss; and Post-Traumatic Stress Disorder affects one in six veterans. These figures do not include the large numbers of veterans with impaired vision, as well as those with mild to moderate traumatic brain injuries. Women veterans are also on the rise, and many have been noted to bring with them unique issues and symptoms associated with experiencing sexual assault in the military.

Most notably, the Post-9/11 GI Bill is changing the face of college campuses. Since the inception of the Veterans Educational Assistance Act of 2008, veterans can receive financial benefits if they pursue an associate's degree or higher. As a result, it is estimated that more than two million veterans returning from the Iraq and Afghanistan wars will enroll in postsecondary education (ACE, 2008). Consequently, as the number of veterans returning to school increases, so does the need for services for those veterans.

Student veterans bring experiences to the classroom which are very different from those of traditional college-aged students. Colleges should collaborate with student veteran groups and "think outside the box" in order to seek out student veterans, since they often will not seek out the support they need on campus. This is mainly because student veterans do not want to be labeled; there are many misconceptions and stereotypes about student veterans, particularly those with disabilities: not all veterans have been in combat, and not all veterans who have served in Iraq or Afghanistan have Post-Traumatic Stress Disorder (PTSD).

Generally, there is not a "one size fits all" approach when it comes to helping disabled student veterans in higher education. Disability service providers in higher education are encountering many unique issues, including disabled veterans who have "fallen through the cracks" because they do not experience disability symptoms until several years after leaving the service (Madaus, Miller & Vance, 2009).

Furthermore, many veterans with disabilities are not only challenged in their adjustment to the college environment; they must also adjust to having acquired a mental and/or physical disability later in their lives. Disability service providers must be prepared to understand that combat veterans with disabilities have challenges only those who have served in combat can truly understand, including their reluctance to seek services and/or disclose a disability. In addition, the documentation brought forth by veterans is often different from what colleges may be seeking, and disability service providers must be willing to accept nontraditional documentation in an effort to eliminate barriers to the utilization of disability services in higher education.

Many veterans are unaware of their rights and responsibilities under the Americans with Disabilities Act Amendment Act because they may have not needed disability services prior to their service in the military (Madaus, Miller & Vance, 2009). Disability service programs must work in close collaboration with VA programs in their areas, and they must seek out opportunities to reach out to various veteran groups, both on and off campus. In addition, disability service personnel must be aware that, just because a veteran is not determined to have a disability by the military, that does not mean that they do not have a disability as defined by Section 504 of the Rehabilitation Act or the ADA Amendments Act. Conversely, veterans must realize that a disability determination by the military does not automatically entitle the veteran to receive academic adjustments in the classroom.

Some disabled veterans also report that disability services personnel need to exhibit their willingness to help a population of students who are not use to utilizing services. This might include assisting veterans who may need to have procedures explained to them and having staff who show a willingness to work patiently with disabled student veterans who are not used to using any type of disability services in higher education.

Depending on the type of disability and documentation presented to a disability service office, accommodations for student veterans with disabilities might include, but are not limited to, the use of assistive listening devices for veterans with hearing loss; assistance with note taking; use of audio devices in the classroom; and/or more lenient attendance policies. Other accommodations include priority seating throughout the classroom, depending on the veteran's needs, as well as accessible seating configurations. Still other accommodations that are often utilized are extended time on tests as well as reduced-distraction testing environments, copies of overhead presentations, and, in some cases, alternative text. Some colleges have gone even further, putting priority registration policies in place for veteran students with disabilities.

Higher education faces many challenges when it comes to talking about disability as part of the diversity discussion. Despite advances precipitated by the Disability Rights Movement, portrayals of individuals with disabilities, including veterans, in literature and popular media are often frozen in time and depict many stereotypes, some of which evoke pity, inspire admiration built out of guilt, or create a character whose physical disability is often portrayed as some type of evil.

In higher education, disability service is now seeing a paradigm shift from the medical model—in which disability is a problem that resides with the individual and is often depicted as a negative that needs to be fixed—to an interactive model, where the disability occurs through the interaction between the individual and society. A disability is neutral (that is, neither negative or positive), and it is the interaction between the individual and society, rather than the individual, that must be altered. Student veterans with disabilities are part of that paradigm shift, one in which we have evolved from a culture where disability is characterized by pity and charity to one that see it from the perspective of civil and human rights.

Disability is an aspect of human experience that crosses all boundaries of race, class, and gender, and it leaves a trail in all societies everywhere. Disability support providers often experience veterans with disabilities—perhaps more than any other group—as students who possess attributes that help them adjust on a daily basis because they must think creatively about how to solve problems and accomplish tasks, making them one of higher education's greatest assets.

Communities of learning are enriched by a wide variety of experiences and perspectives among their students, faculty, and staff, and disability service offices and personnel in higher education often talk about equal access for students with disabilities in the context of inclusion and diversity. Today, the definition of diversity has moved far beyond the legally protected categories that we have grown accustomed to acknowledging, and includes such populations as veterans with disabilities.

Universities should be committed to building diverse campus communities that ensure that all students explore their interests, discover new academic and extracurricular pursuits, and learn from each other. Moreover, education should be accessible to students from a broad range of cultural, ethnic, and economic backgrounds. In particular, veterans with disabilities contribute to the overall "competitive edge" gained by developing a great student body because they demonstrate the ability to adapt to different situations and overcome difficult circumstances. Now, more than ever, college campuses must work together and value human differences in order to provide the kind of quality education students expect when they attend an institution of higher education.

REFERENCES

American Council on Education (2008, November). "Serving those who serve: higher education and America's veterans." http://www.acenet.edu/news-room/Pages/Georgetown-Summit.aspx

Council for Exceptional Children (2005). *Universal design for learning: a guide for teachers and education professionals.* Arlington, VA: Council for Exceptional Children.

Davis, B.G. (1993). *Tools for Teaching.* San Francisco, CA: John Wiley & Sons, Inc.

Madaus, J., Miller, W. & Vance, M.L. (2009). "Veterans with Disabilities in Postsecondary Education." *Journal of Postsecondary Education and Disability*, Vol. 22, No. 1.

Marchione, Marilyn (2012, May). "Iraq, Afghanistan veterans filing for disability benefits at historic rate." Retrieved May 27, 2012 from http://www.huffingtonpost.com/2012/05/27/iraq-afghanistan-veterans-disability-benefits_n_1549436.html

Rose, D.H. & Meyer, A. (2002). *Teaching Every Student in the Digital Age: Universal Design for Learning.* Alexandria, VA: ASCS.

Rothstein, L.F. (1991). "Campuses and the disabled." *Chronicle of Higher Education*, 38, 3, 10.

ALLEN COLEMAN
STUDENT, UTSA

Allen is a nontraditional student who looks far too young to be the father of seven children. Over the past two years, he has juggled a full-time job, course work, and his parenting responsibilities. His honesty about his struggles to meet these demands, along with his genuine concern for others, have helped him to become a valued member of the Veteran Scholars Program and a voice for the value of seeking support and balance at all stages of life.

I had to squint then turn away as the glare of the sun reflected off the acrylic canopy and polished metal body, temporarily blinding me. I had seen this machine only in pictures before. The pictures didn't prepare me for the size and striking beauty of the mechanical marvel in front of and all around me.

Earlier that morning, it took some convincing from my Dad to get me to come to the air show. But, once on the tarmac, I knew I was where I belonged. Most of that day has long been forgotten, but my fascination for military aircraft hasn't. I wasn't alone; my younger brother had also caught the bug. We didn't know it then, but this fascination would consume a large part of our lives, especially the life of my brother.

My dad grew up during World War II, and was influenced by the airplanes of that time. His favorite was the P-51 Mustang. His interest is the only reason we ever went to any air show in the beginning. He had joined the National Guard as a heavy equipment operator, and was fortunate that his unit was never called to Vietnam.

Across the street was another aviation enthusiast; my uncle had joined the Air Force at a young age while the Vietnam conflict was raging. He became a pilot of the F-4 Phantom and flew several missions over Vietnam. By the time I understood what my uncle flew, he was in the Reserves, and the F-4 was being replaced by the next generation of fighters, the F-15 and F-16 in the Air Force, and the F-14 in the Navy. Although he lived just across the street, it was a rare occasion when we ever talked to him. I still regret not taking that opportunity. The only story I recall is of his bombing elephants during the Vietnam War. The Vietnamese would use elephants to pass notes through enemy lines. To stop this communication, some F-4s were used to bomb the elephants. I think my brother was more influenced by my uncle than I was.

As we grew older, we became more interested in the technical aspects of the different aircraft. For birthdays, we asked for Jane's books on military aircraft. They were expensive but full of information. We eventually found our favorites to drool over and debate which one was the best. I chose the F-14 Tomcat, and my brother chose the F-15 Eagle. Up to that moment, I had wanted to be a professional athlete, Formula 1 driver, astronaut, or scientist—the list was massive. Now, the only thing I wanted was to be an aviator for the United States Navy. I would imagine myself climbing up the side of an F-14, stepping into the cockpit, settling into the seat, and then strapping myself into the five-point harness. The imagined pre-flight check was always different, as I would do my best to remember the layout of the cockpit and guess at the controls. The launch from the aircraft carrier had to be the highlight of the whole flight.

My brother had the same intensity for the F-15. We spent hours debating the merits of the two aircraft. I knew the F-15 was more maneuverable, had a better thrust-to-weight ratio, and could be a single-seater, but I would rebut his arguments with the F-14's superior avionics, available weapons, and variable geometric wing configuration. In the end, we didn't change our opinions about which was the superior aircraft, nor of our dreams to fly them.

As I grew older, I became involved in the Boy Scouts of America. We met weekly in a house across the field. A normal Scout meeting would consist of sitting around with a bunch of boys competing for the title of funniest, coolest person in the room. Being somewhat antisocial, I was only annoyed and regretted my involvement. There was so much not to like—the nerdy uniforms, the complicated rules to planning a campout, the constantly competing boys who would pounce on anybody perceived as weak or not cool. I knew it was only a matter of time before I would likely become the target. Not willing to take a chance, I made some lame excuses to my parents and quit after making it to the Tenderfoot ranking.

Filling the weekly time void from quitting Scouts didn't take very long after my brother and I received word of an auxiliary program the Air Force had designed for kids: the Civil Air Patrol. We found there was a unit twenty minutes down the road in Provo, Utah. It wasn't a large unit, but they did have their own Cessna 172. Sold! We quickly joined.

Each week, we would practice formation drills, study for rank advancements, and talk about different military aircraft. Multiple times a year we would have the opportunity to fly in the Cessna 172 to local airports such as Salt Lake International, Spanish Fork, and others. We would take turns in the front seat with a senior member of Civil Air Patrol, flying in and out of the airports.

On one of these flights, we had flown to Salt Lake Airport #2. We switched seating, which rotated me to the front seat. I was to help fly to Salt Lake International Airport. Taking off from the airport was uneventful, and we quickly flew into Salt Lake International airspace. We had headphones to hear the control tower, but I could never understand all the gibberish. I was at the mercy of the pilot.

As we circled around the airport waiting for our turn to land, I carefully held the controls steady. We turned crosswind, preparing for our final approach. Finally, we were able to turn final approach. I had to remember an aviation saying: "You see red, you're dead; you see red over white, you'll be all right; you see white, you'll fly all night."

As we were making our perfect descent, a large 727 flew over the top of us, in front of us, toward the runway. Being fairly naïve, I didn't realize the dangerous situation we were in. The wingtip vortices of the 727 would flow downward and inward, exactly where we were positioned. If we were caught in these vortices, we would be flung uncontrollably through the air toward the rapidly approaching ground. The experience of the senior pilot saved our lives as he pushed for full power, increased altitude, and aborted the landing. He was so calm about the situation we never realized we were in any danger at all.

Civil Air Patrol was a very large part of my early teenage years. Through this program we became friends with many active and retired military personnel, and we became especially close to an Air National Guard Unit. Many times we flew the Canadian-made C-7 Caribou to different air shows, where we would offer our crowd- control services in exchange for free entrance—and a ride in the C-7.

One air show in northern Utah was particularly busy, and was a three-day event rather than the typical two-day show. As we were departing the tarmac in the C-7, the aircraft struggled to change direction. After many attempts to make the turn off the tarmac, the engines finally stopped whirling, and the pilots came back to tell us the bad news: the front landing gear had been stuck in the black goo, which didn't allow the landing gear to turn. After the pilots tried to force the gear to turn, over and over again, one of the rods used to steer the landing gear snapped, rendering the aircraft unable to turn. We sadly waited the three hours for one of the parents to pick us up in a van and drive us back down to our waiting parents.

Through Civil Air Patrol, we also were able to fly in a C-130 to Nellis and Edwards Air Force bases. Although we weren't allowed to leave the aircraft in Nellis, just trying to make out the different shapes through the small circular windows was as exciting as seeing the figures themselves. Once we landed at Edwards Air Force Base in California, we were able to take tours of different aircraft (including the A-10, F-16, and F-111), the NASA testing center, and other fascinating things. One summer I was able to camp at an Army base near the foothills of Lehi, Utah, where we were able to fly in a UH-60 through the canyons. I was seated on the outermost seat looking outward. I requested that the door remain open, which became one of the thrills of my life.

As I grew older, I lost interest in the "nerdiness" of Civil Air Patrol, so I quit and got more involved in high school life. My interest in the F-14 slightly diminished due to the reality of what it would take to actually fly an F-14. My brother was still interested in flying an F-15, but he had a new interest in "war games." He had a couple of friends who would dress in camouflage pants and shirts, paint their faces, and "shoot" each other with fake guns. They took it so far as to camp up in the mountains, on cliffs, in forests, anywhere to make the war games more realistic and adventurous for them. He also took his studying seriously, which would help him immensely in his future. Unfortunately, I didn't do the same, which would prevent me from realizing my own dream.

After high school graduation, I was again serious about flying an F-14, so I visited the recruiting offices for the Navy, Air Force, and Army. After talking to recruiters from all three branches, I narrowed it down to the Navy, as I was "promised" a maintenance crew chief slot that would lead to mu becoming a pilot, or so the recruiter told me.

I agreed to take some military assessments, which concluded that I had the aptitude for a maintenance crew chief position. A time was set to sign the papers that would make me a member of the United States Navy. The week before the signing day, I began to have second thoughts. To be certain this decision would not be one I'd regret, I discussed my reservations with a couple of veterans. I learned from them that the maintenance crew chief position would not lead to an aviator position, and I had been lied to by the recruiter.

The day came. As I drove to the recruiter's office, thoughts were racing through my head. The thirty-minute drive stretched to agonizing hours, or so it seemed. Approaching the office door, I still hadn't made up my mind. I entered through the doors, into the office of the recruiter, and sat in the seat in front of his desk. He turned the papers in front of me, handed me a pen with a large smile, and waited.

Suddenly, a stream of words started spewing from my mouth. It was like an out-of-body experience, hearing myself speaking to the recruiter. I politely declined, explaining that my future plans to serve as a missionary for my church the following year would interfere with my military plans. And, upon returning to Utah after completing my two-year mission, I may find that my interests were totally different. The recruiter, enraged, picked up the pen, flung it across the room, threw the papers off the desk, and proceeded to yell at me. I can't remember what was said, but I felt calm, and I knew that was the best decision for me.

I spent the summer working to save money for my missionary service. My younger brother was finishing his senior year of high school, and was now talking about being an Army Ranger. After he graduated from high school, my parents agreed to sign him up for the Army; he was just seventeen, so my parents' signatures were required.

The compromise was the contract. It was an eight-year contract with a two-year leave of absence allowed any time during those eight years. This was to allow my brother to serve as a missionary for two years, if he chose to. Both sides agreed, and the contract was signed.

Before my brother signed the papers, I had already departed to Stockholm, Sweden to start my two-year missionary service. The only form of communication between us was in-frequent letters. Through our correspondence, I learned he had signed up for Special Forces training, the elite special operations group in the Army. As he explained it to me, to become a member of the Special Forces, you endured twenty-four months of training programs. If, at any point during these twenty-four months, you failed one of the programs, or were injured, you couldn't start back where you left off; you had to start the full twenty-four months again.

I was about eight months into my mission service when I received a letter from my brother explaining an unfortunate event. During an exercise, he was the demolitions engineer, and was assigned to carry the radio. They were taken in a C-141 and flown to an unknown destination.

Once they reached the destination, they were given a map and shown the location where they were to meet in three days. They were to reach the point individually.

The normal pack weight for him was eighty to 120 pounds. This exercise was no different. He landed in mountainous terrain, which he had experienced as a youth many times. The first task was to determine his location, then start towards the end destination. He quickly found his bearings and started toward his destination. On the second day, as he was descending the mountain, he stepped incorrectly on a tree root, breaking his ankle. After struggling for many hours, he soon realized he would not be able to make the destination in the given time. He descended to a canyon road and found a ride to the end, knowing he failed. He was shipped home to heal from his wounds, and faced a decision: should he start the twenty-four months over, or serve a mission?

After many days, he decided a mission service was his best option. He was sent to Kiev, Ukraine to serve as one of the first LDS missionaries in that new country. Over the next two years, he became fluent in Russian, and then returned home to Utah. He joined the National Guard linguistics unit (Russian speaking), enrolled in the local university, and earned a bachelor's degree in Russian. During these four years, his interest in flying the F-15 returned.

His tenacious, persistent personality paid off with recommendations from a senator, several veterans, and local leaders to transfer to the Air Force pilot training program. Earning a spot to fly an F-15 was a tall order, but he was determined. After many years of training and waiting, his dream became reality, and he was assigned to Mountain Home Air Base outside of Boise, Idaho, flying his long–fought-for dream, the F-15. He was the only pilot I know who had jump wings attached to his flight suit. Uncertain glares and questions from members of the Army were common.

He eventually got out of the Air Force to move back with family in Texas. By that time, he had two kids and two brothers in the San Antonio area, and his wife is from Del Rio, so the stress of moving every two to three years was too much. He was honorably discharged as a major in the Air Force, and is now working for the government, running the flight simulator program at Randolph Air Force Base in San Antonio.

Looking back at our youth, I realize his success in the military was achieved through his diligent study habits, persistent behavior, and his practice of keeping his eye on his goals. I admire him and his achievements, both in the military and the academic world. These characteristics, along with the habits he acquired in the military, are the reasons for his success today, as an employee, father, husband, and brother. He reminds me that I can do anything I set my mind to do. It takes hard work and perseverance.

His example, and those of many other veterans, has inspired me to partner with veterans in the academic environment. As a member of the Veteran Scholars Program, I have worked with both veteran and nonveteran students to identify the stressors common to veterans and to develop a series of modules—tailored for veteran students—that deal with stress management, coping, and learning to understand the university. Veterans have willingly placed their lives in danger for their country. Whether we agree or disagree with the politics of war and national defense, our veterans deserve a quality education and any program that will assure their successful completion and integration back into the civilian world.

Many traditional students on campus do not know who the veterans are, nor do they know the experience these veterans possess. Veterans' leadership skills, discipline, and persistence would prove very helpful in the context of mentoring young, traditional students. Veterans can be an important piece of the academic puzzle if the pieces are placed in the correct location and not forgotten or lost.

CATHERYN ORIHUELA
MS PSYCHOLOGY, UTSA

Catheryn is a former teacher, working mother, and graduate student who has experience teaching stress management and coping techniques to families of military members. As a founding member of the Veteran Scholars Research group, she was always willing to help others. When she found out that a student vet had lost his housing, she got on the phone and found him an affordable alternative situation. She has now completing her MS in Psychology and has started a PhD program in Psychology at the University of Alabama.

THE CIVILIAN

My involvement with student veterans has been an evolving process, beginning over two years ago when I was still an elementary teacher. Although I had many rewarding experiences over the years with students, parents, and colleagues, I was interested in returning to graduate school to pursue a career as an experimental psychologist. I had always had an interest in psychology, and have had plenty of opportunities to explore psychological issues related to child and adult behavior.

About that same time, there were several families in our school who had family members deployed to support the conflict in the Middle East. Although all of these men and women arrived home safely, I was deeply moved by the effect that deployment had on the family members left at home. The wife or husband was left to take care of the children and home, many times while working a full-time job. When I interacted with the parents, they were always positive, but the strain was obvious.

Communication with the deployed spouse was not always consistent or reliable, and family members at home were not always aware of the exact location of their loved one. Just after a deployment, the children in the family spoke about how they missed their parent, while the very young ones were more clingy and fussy. It made me understand that this is a population that deserves our attention. We need to study and understand the very special needs of the military, which includes the family members.

As I began to think about a new career, I felt that I could create a niche for myself by studying the issues that are unique to today's military population. Having a greater understanding of psychological illnesses, such as Post-Traumatic Stress Disorder (PTSD) and depression, as well as the effects of physical trauma, such as TBI and amputation, can lead to better outcomes for those who experience these issues post-deployment.

After resigning from my teaching position, I enrolled at the University of Texas at San Antonio (UTSA) and immediately found a position at UTHSCSA as a facilitator for a small feasibility study that offered a nine-week stress management program for caregivers of Wounded Warriors. That position opened my eyes to a completely different side of the military: the family members. Having already seen how deployment affects an entire family, I was struck when I saw the effects of caring for someone who was seriously wounded in combat. Most of the participants were female spouses who provided daily care for their loved ones who had suffered amputations, PTSD, severe depression, alcohol and drug addiction, debilitating pain, traumatic brain injuries, or some combination of these, often occurring at the same time.

These family members were under enormous stress as they managed the new responsibility of caring for someone who is severely injured. Enduring the med board process, transitioning into civilian status, and navigating Department of Veterans Affairs (VA) benefits were frustrating and exhausting. They themselves struggled with depression and anxiety, felt overwhelmed with responsibilities, and suppressed anger and resentment toward their situation. They were conflicted with their spirituality and felt a loss of self.

Throughout the nine weeks, we helped participants identify specific stressors and understand how the body responds to stress, and we taught them relaxation techniques to better cope with their stressors. An added and unexpected benefit of the group was the support that they gained from each other. When I first began my job, I was apprehensive about stepping into the military culture, completely ignorant of basic lingo such as PCS and other military terms. However, I was warmly received as someone who was willing to listen and committed to help.

This past year has taught me that there are numerous issues that are affecting our military service members: What are the effects of combat and multiple deployments? Who is at risk for psychological illness? How do we adequately care for injured veterans? How can we better prepare them for transition to civilian life? How can we better support families? Research in these fields is imperative in answering these questions.

JOE DECRISTOFORO
ASSOCIATE VICE PRESIDENT AND UNIVERSITY REGISTRAR

Joe DeCristoforo has been involved in higher education opportunities for approximately thirty-five years, in five different states and as many universities. He went from graduate assistant in the Career Planning and Placement Office at the University of Florida, to Assistant Director of Admissions and Assistant Registrar at Kennesaw State College, to Assistant Director of Records at Georgia Tech, then to Registrar at both Indiana University of Pennsylvania and the University of Toledo.

He has three degrees from the University of Florida (a bachelor's degree in English and two graduate degrees in counselor education), and earned a Doctor of Philosophy degree from Georgia State University in research, measurement, and statistics in 1992. He is currently Associate Vice President and University Registrar at UTSA, and has a daughter who is serving in the US Navy.

ESTABLISHING A VETSUCCESS ON CAMPUS PROGRAM AT THE UNIVERSITY OF TEXAS AT SAN ANTONIO

Although I was never in the military myself, my father was a career Air Force master sergeant and World War II veteran, my grandfather was a Navy sailor, and my daughter is currently serving in the US Navy, stationed at the Pentagon as a Lieutenant and part of the Secretary of the Navy Advisory Panel Staff, so the military has always been a major influence in my life.

I am the registrar at the University of Texas at San Antonio (UTSA), and my office certifies our student veterans so they can receive their benefits from the Department of Veterans Affairs (VA). When the new GI Bill was established, our student veteran population nearly doubled overnight, and our office went from certifying nine hundred veterans and their dependents in the 2008/2009 academic year to more than eighteen hundred in the 2012/2013 academic year. As a result, in 2011 I was asked to establish and cochair a university standing committee, the Veteran Services Advisory Committee (VSAC), to help smooth the transition for our student veterans from military to college life, and to help develop streamlined processes that moved them forward to graduation.

In July 2011, during the first functioning year for our VSAC committee, the Veterans Administration sent me a notice inviting our university to compete to have a VetSuccess on Campus (VSOC) program here at UTSA. I called the contact on the notice and learned that they had sent out approximately forty-five invitations to institutions that had some of the largest numbers of student veterans on college and university campuses.

We were given a sample of the memorandum of understanding (MOU) they had been using at other institutions during the VA's initial startup pilots, and we were asked to send any comments or observations back to the VA if we were interested in becoming a part of this new initiative. Also during my conversation with my VA contact, I learned that a key part of this initiative, hosting a VA vocational rehabilitation counselor on your campus, involved securing a closed office space for the counselor.

The VetSuccess on Campus program was piloted initially at the University of South Florida campus in 2009, and quickly expanded the next year to San Diego State University and Cleveland State University. At the time of this writing, there are thirty-two colleges and universities participating in this program, including UTSA. However, this number is scheduled to increase to sixty-two programs in the next few months.

The first thing I did at UTSA was to get the green light from my supervisor, the Vice President of Student Affairs, Dr. Gage Paine; next, I met with the VSAC committee and was given complete support to move forward as fast as possible. After meeting with UTSA attorneys, we sent our list of questions regarding the current MOU in September 2011.

A few months passed, and we never heard another thing from the VA. I called in November 2011 and talked with my contact at the VA's central office. All I learned at that time was that it was still under review, and that we would hear something eventually. No timetable at all was given.

In mid-January 2012, I got an e-mail from Ms. Cassie Abbott, the assistant VRE officer, Houston Regional Office, who told us that we were approved for a VetSuccess on Campus counselor, and that we needed to meet soon to discuss these events and develop a plan to move forward.

We invited Ms. Abbott to our next VetSuccess meeting, where we met her and the vocational rehabilitation counselor assigned to UTSA, J. Michael Silva. The only major hurdles we needed to overcome at that point were getting a signed MOU and providing a private office for Mr. Silva.

Regarding the private office, I consulted again with my VPSA, and she told me to move forward with a work order to obtain a cost estimate for two private offices—one for Mr. Silva, and a second one in case the VA's Hospital Administration area decided to send a representative as well.

I mentioned to Ms. Abbott during our initial meeting that we had sent in the questions from our UTSA attorneys (about three pages) back in September 2011, six months earlier, and had never heard anything back from the VA. This issue led to a telephone conference call meeting in February 2012 between representatives from the VA Central Office, representatives from the VA Houston Regional Office, and several staff from UTSA. It seemed that most of the questions relating to the MOU were either in the technical, computer technology and computer security areas, or dealt with legal issues relating to FERPA and other areas.

Over the next several months, I worked on getting the MOU approved. From time to time, a legal issue would surface that seemed to place UTSA at risk in some way. When this occurred, I would consult with the Vice President of Student Affairs, and we would discuss the legal ramifications of moving forward with the MOU. In each instance, Dr. Paine decided that the risk was minimal and did not warrant halting the initiative. These issues were part of the general MOU contract that every college or university had to agree to in order to become part of the VetSuccess on Campus program. Dr. Paine felt that the benefit of having a full-time VA vocational rehabilitation counselor on campus to assist our student veterans was of the utmost importance, and she would stand by her decision.

The technical, computer-related issues, however, were much harder to get resolved. In April 2012, we had sent a list of approximately six questions for the VA's computer staff and its attorneys to clarify; most involved security and clarifications of computer protocols that we were required to follow, even though we did not have any access at all to any of the VA-specific computer handbooks referenced in the MOU. Our security staff felt that they were being asked to agree to follow certain computer protocols, even though they had no idea what these protocols required or consisted of.

While this was happening, the cost estimate came back, indicating that it would cost approximately $50,000 to build two private, soundproof offices for the VA counselors. Even though we were not given a solid indication by the VA that we would be assigned two counselors, we decided to build both offices, and if it turned out that we received only one counselor, we would use the extra office for other purposes.

A few weeks after construction started, we received word that the VR & E area would be allowed to give us two counselors after all, based on the very high numbers of student veterans on our campus, so this worked out really well.

In order to move the MOU forward, it was suggested that I contact the General Counsel of the VA, who was in charge of the MOU document. Before I contacted him, I called several colleges and universities across the country and talked to the respective main MOU contact who was responsible for coordinating things in order to get the MOU signed to bring the VA staff to each campus.

During these discussions, I learned that rarely did the VA bend on any of the MOU rules and regulations. In all of the calls I made, I only recall hearing of only one instance in which the VA modified the MOU to accommodate the needs of one of the institutions. There was one institution that was able to get the MOU signed and have a vocational rehabilitation counselor on their campus in a few short months, although it seemed that the average time was in the six-to-eight-month timeframe. There were a couple of institutions that took more than a year from the date they started discussing the MOU before it was finally signed and authorized, and I was hoping that we would not fall into that category. I even found one institution that took about a year to approve the MOU, though they allowed the vocational rehabilitation counselor to have an interim office on their campus and help their student veterans while the details of the MOU were worked out behind the scenes.

I eventually talked with the VA General Counsel, who was extremely understanding and accommodating. The VA actually revised their MOU and struck out several of the areas of concern named by our computer security staff on the MOU itself. While this was happening, our computer security staff said that they would be willing to drop most of their concerns in an effort to get the MOU signed. I was almost in a state of disbelief that after several months of negotiations, two apparently immovable forces had become more flexible and accommodating almost overnight.

This occurred at the beginning of the summer term, so I thought we were well on our way toward getting this signed before the end of summer so the counselors could get started prior to the Fall 2012 term rush. However, I made a strategic error in judgment: I should have gotten the contractual attorneys involved in this process much earlier. Up until that time, I had only been operating with the legal counsel of our university, but there is another legal area on our campus that gives final signature approval of any contracts, agreements, or similar legal-type documents, such as memoranda of understandings.

I called a meeting between the legal counsel I had been working with and the contractual attorneys to review any new issues that may have developed. Legal questions similar to those that had come up months earlier came up again, though essentially most of these were resolved; the VPSA, whose area would be responsible for hosting these two VA counselors, was consistent in waiving these concerns in the interest of securing two VA counselors to help our student veterans.

After a few weeks, I was on my summer vacation on the Copano Bay fishing pier in Rockport, Texas, with a fishing rod in my hands when I heard my iPhone e-mail alert sound and checked my messages. The e-mail, forwarded to me from the contractual attorneys, contained questions about the MOU that needed clarification from the VA's legal counsel. I immediately forwarded the message to my contacts with the VA in Houston to forward on to the Central Office legal staff for review. This was on July 9, 2012.

Several weeks later, we got another revised MOU from the VA, though this one struck out the "hold harmless" indemnification clause that UTSA's legal counsel had added to the MOU back when it was initially sent, in September 2011, to be reviewed. This clause had been in every MOU that we sent back and forth since the beginning, and, at this late stage of the game, it suddenly became an issue. Much discussion went back and forth regarding this question, but eventually it was decided by the contractual attorneys that the risk was really low to our university, and UTSA accepted its removal from the document.

Ultimately, the MOU was finally approved and signed by all parties. When I got initial word of this via an e-mail notice (on September 18, 2012, at 9:54 a.m., from Ms. Cassie Abbott, to be precise), I did several high-fives with others on our campus who had worked through this process with me.

The two VA vocational rehabilitation counselors, Wendy Foster and J. Michael Silva, moved into their offices on September 24, 2012. We had a reception in their honor, and on September 27, 2012, they and some top VA officials from the Houston Regional Office met with our President, Dr. Ricardo Romo.

In many ways, we treat our VA counselors in the same way that we treat our regular office staff. Whenever they need any office supplies, they just come to our office and pick up what they need on their own. While the VA has supplied their computer, we have given them a login to our Student Information System so that they can check on any student veteran and retrieve whatever information they feel is necessary to assist the student.

While the VA staff has access to our student database, we determined early on not to request the same type of access to the VA database for our staff. It was quite a challenge getting through the MOU without asking for this access, and whenever our veteran certification staff has questions, the two VA counselors work with them expeditiously to give them answers from the VA system.

The office space where the two VA counselors are located is in our Veteran Certification office. We have three full-time staff at the main campus and one full-time certification staff at our downtown campus. A year before the two VA counselors joined our campus, we had doubled our initial Veteran Certification office at a cost of approximately $50,000. This renovation expense, when combined with the construction of two soundproof private offices for our VA friends, means that we have spent more than $100,000 in a one-year period to make our facilities more accommodating to our staff so that they, in turn, can have more space to help our student veterans. Eventually, we are hoping to relocate our office staff to a larger area where services of a "one-stop shop" can be combined with a student veteran lounge.

We try to include Wendy and J. Michael in all office functions. Officially, they do not report to the Registrar's office, but since they are housed in an office area with our staff and share the same goal of serving our student veterans, we feel they are part of our community. They attend our staff meetings when they can, and this past summer they attended our all-day, all-office retreat. They participate in our monthly staff success meetings, and this year Wendy is actually a leader of her own staff success group.

Our entire campus has reached out to our VA counselors, and now that we have had them here for a year, we wonder just where in the world we would be without them. In the 365 days that make up a year, they have seen more than two thousand students between the two of them.

Early on, when funds had not been identified for the construction of their offices, our University Career Center Director, Audrey Magnuson, volunteered to loan the VA Counselors one or two of her interview rooms as temporary office space until their offices were built. However, due to the delays in getting the MOU signed, the office construction finished several months prior to their starting anyway, so we never really needed this option, although it was a welcome relief at the time.

I cannot offer enough thanks for Cassie Abbott and Kelley Shupak, from the VA Houston Regional Office, for all of the assistance they have provided during the period when our lives intersected with the sole objective of bringing skilled VA counselors to our campus to help our student veterans. I am guessing that in the year that it took to bring them to our campus, I sent and received probably more than a thousand e-mails related to this goal, and probably half of these e-mails mentioned Cassie and Kelley somewhere. They were tireless and always optimistic, and knew from the get-go how valuable their staff would be to our students in this environment—and I would say that, if anything, their staff has somehow managed to even exceed our high expectations.

MARY MCNAUGHTON-CASSILL

PROFESSOR OF CLINICAL PSYCHOLOGY

CAN DOGS AND CATS GET ALONG AND COMPLEMENT EACH OTHER?

Although I never served in the military, I grew up in San Diego, California, and have spent most of my adult life in San Antonio, Texas. Among other things, both cities have a strong military presence and pride themselves on their support for service members. As a child, I didn't understand why my friend's fathers were often gone for months at a time, but I was jealous of the beautiful Japanese dolls and carved boxes they brought when they came home. Like most San Diegans of the era, my family waited every year for the annual Blue Angels Air Show. By the time I was in college at the University of California at Santa Barbara, I was accustomed to driving through Camp Pendleton on my way to and from school, squinting at both the ocean and the mountains to see if the Marines were conducting training exercises.

I didn't have the opportunity to work with veterans professionally until I started teaching part-time at a community college in San Diego. When taking classes such as Psychology and Health and Behavior Modification, veterans often spoke up about their struggles to adjust to civilian life. I remember one student who came up to me after class to tell me how embarrassed he once felt about diving under his desk during a thunderstorm.

When I later returned to graduate school at the University of California San Diego/San Diego State University Clinical Psychology program, I actually started interacting with veterans on a professional level, at the San Diego Veterans Association Medical Center. After graduating, I also spent a year at the VA as a staff psychologist working in an outpatient program as well as with patients who had experienced spinal cord injuries. As a result, I had the opportunity to talk with veterans who had served in World War II, Korea, Vietnam, and the Middle East.

Interestingly, despite differences in their war experiences and the support they were offered for their efforts when they came home, their stories were similar. The civilian world expected them to come back from their life-changing experiences unchanged and to quickly fit back into their prior lives. Although most veterans do successfully readjust, they often struggle to reconcile their wartime experiences with civilian life.

In addition, they face challenges in rebuilding or creating their careers, as well as reconnecting with family and friends. Often they are also be dealing with physical (Helmer et al., 2007) and psychological (Hoge, Castro, Messer, McGurk, Cotting, & Koffman, 2004) issues related to their service. For example, one Vietnam veteran told me about his decades-long struggle to avoid the smell of wet grass, which reminded him of being stranded in the jungle in Vietnam.

It is not unusual for veterans to find that they face a tough job market, despite their success in the military. In order to cope, many choose to use their GI benefits to either attend school themselves or, when possible, to support family members who wish to do so. While the financial benefits of the GI bill make this possible, both veterans and universities are finding that the needs of such individuals vary from those of traditional students (Cook & Kim, 2009).

Returning veterans, by definition, are not coming to college straight out of high school. This means they are older than the average freshman. In addition, as a result of their military experience, they have unique skill sets and life experiences that affect their approach to school (Ackerman, DiRamio, & Mitchell, 2009). Veterans also vary from each other in terms of their early education and preparation for school. Some wonder if they can perform academically after being out of school for long periods of time. Others are concerned because they have attended more than one college during their military careers.

Demographically, many military veterans are from ethnic groups which are underrepresented in college (Armor and Gilroy, 2010) and/or are first-generation college students, and so don't come from families who automatically know how to help them succeed; frequently, the promise of college was one reason for joining the military in the first place. Further complicating the situation is the fact that many veterans are also experiencing significant mental health issues, including severe anxiety, depression, suicidal thoughts, and PTSD (Rudd, Goulding, & Bryan (2011).

In short, although many veterans are older than traditional students and have been out of school for a while, they are highly motivated to succeed academically. Nevertheless, many veterans find that the demands of college differ significantly from the demands of military service and that they need to develop new academic skill sets in order to manage college-level work.

I frequently speak with student veterans who admit that they initially underestimated the stress of attending school. Often they wonder how something as seemingly different from combat as taking an exam or writing a paper can be so stressful. In addition, they often find it hard to ask for help. In practice, for many veterans, going to school is like being an exchange student in a foreign country. They don't know the language, the rules, or the customs, and they aren't sure how to figure out what they need to do.

Ironically, their familiarity with and entrenchment in military culture may make it even harder to adjust to life in academia. For instance, the military fosters common values and goals which include toughness, control, and taking action. In addition, the chain of command is based on a clearly delineated hierarchy, authority is mandated, and uniforms are used to signal people's position in the organization. Each time people are assigned to a new duty station they are given specific training and instructions; as a whole, the military fosters social support and camaraderie.

By contrast, academics tend to take pride in thinking independently and in pursuing individual goals. While talking to a group of veterans, I once mentioned that the structure of the military reminded me of a wolf pack, while universities more closely resemble a colony of cats. That imagery stuck, and when they knew I was going to give a talk about veteran students, they always reminded me not to forget to mention the dogs and cats.

Another difference that frequently disorients veterans is that, at the typical university, people move up and down in the administrative hierarchy and can rarely be recognized by their attire; I have had veteran students tell me that they initially failed to recognize that the person in shorts and sandals who wandered into the classroom was actually the professor until he started talking. Furthermore, students are often in competition with each other for grades, as opposed to working together to achieve a common goal.

Although most universities are just starting to realize that veterans are not typical traditional students and would benefit from veteran-specific orientations and academic support programs, it is going to take time to address the gaps between the ways veterans and academics view the world. Veterans can contribute to the process by speaking up about their points of view and taking on campus leadership roles. In doing so they enrich both their own and the educational experiences of those around them. The bottom line is that most veterans don't want us to make school easier or more like the military. They simply want us to help them figure out what they need to do to survive and thrive in an academic setting.

In turn, veterans need to realize that they can enrich the campus, and the educational experiences of those around them, by speaking up about their points of view and taking on campus leadership roles. The bottom line is that most veterans don't want us to make school easier or more like the military. They simply want us to help them figure out what they need to do to survive and thrive in an academic setting.

At UTSA we have created a formal committee to address the needs of student veterans, and are working to improve the services we offer. Ongoing efforts range from expanding our Veterans Services Office to developing veteran-specific orientation programming (programs) and supporting the Veteran Student Association.

In the past several years I have been working with a group of both veteran and nonveteran psychology students to collect data on the veteran student experience at UTSA, and to develop a series of student-led workshops to be offered to incoming veterans to ease their transition to college. The topics include time management, academic skills, transferring your leadership skills to a university setting, finding mentors, and managing stress. This research team voted to call themselves the Veteran Scholars Program, and have participated in numerous discussions on campus about veterans' issues. They also conducted a panel discussion at the Southwestern Psychological Association Meeting held in San Antonio, Texas in 2014. An artistic member of the group has even designed a logo and received permission from both the US military and UTSA to create special coins to be handed out to UTSA veterans; this resembles the military tradition of commemorating achievements with specially designed coins. The goals of the group are explicitly to help veterans develop identities as students and scholars while still honoring their military experiences and accomplishments.

Given the value of a college education in today's world and the debt we owe our veterans for their service to this country, it would seem important for all of us to increase our understanding of the veteran college experience. This in turn will enable us to figure out how best to help our student veterans transition from the military, to college, to their professional lives successfully. I can still picture the active-duty student who stood in the doorway of my office and told me that he was more "scared to go to college then to go back to war." We need to change that perception, student by student.

CPSIA information can be obtained
at www.ICGtesting.com
Printed in the USA
FSOW02n1835210416
19552FS

9 781626 616059